Personal Faith with a Passion

How to Know What You Really Believe

Ray Dykes

Personal Faith with a Passion:
How to Know What You Really Believe

Published in 2003 by Pair'o'Docs Press,
9205 Lansbrook Lane, Oklahoma City, Oklahoma 73132

Copyright © 2003
by Pair'o'Docs Press

All rights reserved. Printed in the United States of America.
No part of this book may be used or reproduced in any manner whatsoever without written permission, except in the case of brief quotations embodied in articles and reviews.
For more information, contact Pair'o'Docs Press at the above address

ISBN - 0-9723884-1-9

Acknowledgments

This book is dedicated to
Donna Stokes Dykes,
my wife,
the love of my life,
my editor
and the best teacher of
Hebrew Bible on the planet.

I acknowledge the straw
given to me by my father,
Ray Dykes,
(1909-2000)
who was a faithful Abraham,
going whither he knew not,
following the call of God.

I am indebted to
Christine Wicker,
author of *God Knows My Heart*
and reporter for *The Dallas Morning News*,
who started me on this project.

Thanks to my son,
Dave Dykes,
for his excellent work
with cover design and book layout.

Thanks to my friend,
Jane Buchanan,
for her transcription service.

Introducing
Personal Faith with a Passion

It is about . . .

- Teaching and modeling a simple and proven technique to combine personal experience with religious information and showing how to use the result to build personal faith

- Discerning which religious information works for each person

- Validating religious information with personal experience and hope

- Constructing a "spiritual house of faith"

- Learning that there are belief options available in religious information, and what some of the options are

- Understanding the difference between faith and fact

- Declaring spiritual independence in the face of religious tyranny

- Accepting the freedom to question, doubt or clarify long-held beliefs

- Giving Christian laity the "third license of the Reformation"

- Building a personal Christian faith, which can be expressed consciously and humbly

- Sharing personal faith appropriately with children and grandchildren

- Believing with a passion, using faith in every aspect of life and embracing faith-building as a life-long task

It is NOT about . . .

- Creating a "Do-It-Yourself" religion

- Promoting a bunch of wild-eyed sectarians

- Acquiring individualistic, "feel good" faith, devoid of religious information and the spiritual wisdom of the ages

Table of Contents

Prologue 13
    Why it is important to have personal faith with a passion

Introduction 17
    How to build your spiritual house of faith

Section A 21
    Massaging Your Clay
    To Understand Your Spiritual Experiences

    Chapter 1. 25
        In whose face have you seen the face of God?
    Chapter 2. 33
        Where have you experienced God in nature and life events?
    Chapter 3. 41
        Which stories about God-like characters told you about God?
    Chapter 4. 49
        How do you pray and what do you say when you pray?

Section B 59
    Sorting Through Old Straw
    For Spiritual Messages From Your Past

    Chapter 5. 61
        Who told you that?
    Chapter 6. 67
        Have you looked at the words of the spiritual songs you sang?

Section C 73
    Gathering New Straw
    From Current Spiritual Messages

    Chapter 7. 75
        Does the Bible have errors and contradictions,
        and what difference does it make?
    Chapter 8. 83
        Are there problems with Jesus being "the divine Son of God?"
    Chapter 9. 91
        Is it enough for Jesus to be a human Messiah?
    Chapter 10. 101
        Where in the world did Holy Spirit come from?

Chapter 11. 107
    Is it necessary to believe in the Trinity?
Chapter 12. 113
    Is there only one concept of the will of God?

Section D 119
Mixing Clay and Straw Together to Mold Belief Bricks
And Understanding How Belief Bricks Relate to Daily Experiences

Chapter 13. 121
    What is human nature? When does human life begin and end?
Chapter 14. 129
    How do you know what's right and wrong?
Chapter 15. 135
    Chaos and evil: did the Devil do it?
Chapter 16. 141
    Are you saved? Where did heaven and hell go?
    Is there going to be a Judgment Day?
    Where do you go from here?
Chapter 17. 151
    Depression, despair, mid-life crisis, the
    death of the human spirit: Is that a spiritual event?
Chapter 18. 157
    Hope, metamorphosis, new life, the
    resurrection of the human spirit: Is that a spiritual event?
Chapter 19. 163
    Is it time to fire your old God?

Section E 167
Allowing Your Belief Bricks
To Express Themselves

Chapter 20. 169
    How can you consciously express what you believe
    about the nature of God?
Chapter 21. 175
    How can you express your faith to children?

Epilogue 179
What Do You Believe So Passionately that You
Would Give Up Everything You Own for It Right Now?

PERSONAL FAITH WITH A PASSION:
How to Know What You Really Believe
by Ray Dykes

PROLOGUE
No matter how hard you work on your mind to learn,
No matter how hard you work on your body to look good,
No matter how hard you work on your psyche to feel good,
No matter how hard you work on your career to make money,
If you don't work on your spiritual life,
Life at its best will always be beyond your grasp.
But . . .
The more you bring your personal faith to conscious expression,
The better you can know yourself and understand yourself,
The better you can accept yourself and love yourself.
The better you love yourself,
The more likely you are to love another person unconditionally,
And to love God more, as you understand God.
Then you can live life at its best.
Then you can truly experience Personal Faith with a Passion.

The better you know what you believe about God, the better you know who you are. You need self-understanding, a healthy self-concept, a positive identity, and your conscious faith is the key to all that. When your faith has integrity with the way you live your life, you have meaning and purpose in your life. With a carefully constructed personal faith, you can handle the crises of life and experience growth even in the midst of difficulties.

In the process of building your faith, you learn the true, profound meaning of freedom and responsibility. When you know you have the freedom to build and rebuild your own theology, you know you must give others the same freedom. When you build your faith, you know that it is your responsibility to "work out (your) salvation with a sense of awe," (Philippians 2:12) in partnership with God, one day at a time. When you accept responsibility for what you believe, you become aware that spiritual craziness can lead to psychotic and anti-social behavior. When you experience the difficulty of building your own faith, you learn the real meaning of humility and you cannot be spiritually arrogant toward another pilgrim.

At issue is your identity, your effectiveness as a human being, your ability to establish covenant relationships, your ability to cope with the best and the worst of life, your knowing the meaning and purpose of your life, your freedom and responsibility, and your ability to walk humbly with your God and family and friends. In short, your spiritual life is at issue. There is nothing more important than your spiritual life. Building your own faith is the most important thing you will ever do. That makes this book worth reading and this task worth doing.

Most people don't know what they believe about spiritual matters. Some know what they've been told to believe. Some know what they're expected to believe. However, when they run into the spiritual wall of despair in the "dark night of the soul," most don't know how to begin to construct a faith that includes meaning and purpose. When they need to describe their concept of God, or when they want to talk about their faith with others, including children, they don't know how to express what they believe.

Joe's life was football. He was bred to be a quarterback, tall and sturdy, with great instincts and a quick ball release. Everybody in his Texas hometown was proud of him when he was named High School All-American after leading his team to win the state championship. Joe was active in his church and the Fellowship of Christian Athletes. He accepted the "standard" faith of his community without thinking about it.

College football was good for Joe, except for the concussions he suffered while being sacked by defensive linemen. In the bowl game at the end of the season of his senior year, he sustained a serious neck injury and a major concussion when he was slammed to the artificial turf. The doctors told him he was through with football. Instead of a promising career in the NFL, he lost his life's purpose.

After a decade of wallowing in self-pity and despair, Joe discovered one week-end at a workshop that he could find a new passion in life by building his own faith. Using the same determination that had made him a top quarterback, he constructed a faith that he could claim as his own, a faith that has given him new meaning and purpose and zeal for life.

Here is a book that teaches people how to bring their own personal faith to conscious expression. This book supplies you with a technique to build your own faith never before made available. This technique is experientially-based and has been taught personally to many people.

This book may function for you and future generations as a "Declaration of Spiritual Independence." There have always been religious tyrants in the land, doing their best to suppress spiritual independence by telling people what they are supposed to believe. Religious tyranny need no longer be the order of the day. No longer do people need to go to priest, pastor, or minister to be told what to believe. No longer does theology have to be the exclusive purview of the professional religious elite. Theological freedom and spiritual independence have been made possible by the simple technique contained in this book.

Personal Faith with a Passion makes possible the beginning of a new "Spiritual Reformation." The Protestant Reformation of the 1500's gave Christian laity a license to read the Bible for themselves and a second license to pray to God directly. Before that, they had to go to their priests to find out what the Bible said, since it was written in Latin, which only the priests could read. Also, they presented their prayer requests to priests who interceded with God on their behalf. Now, here's a book that gives all people everywhere the third license, the license to discover what they really believe and express that faith with passion, commitment and confidence.

"Now faith is the assurance of things hoped for, the conviction of things not seen," according to a verse in the New Testament Letter to the Hebrews (11:1). Faith can be conscious and/or unconscious and is never provable, never factual. Indeed, the opposite of faith is fact, not doubt. Doubt is an integral part of faith. They are two sides of the same coin, because whatever is not doubt-able is not faith-able. Theology, then, is the conscious expression of faith, and part of the content of your theology is that which is unseen, for which you hope. The "assurance" is by way of saying that you can be sure of that which you believe, and you can come to know that as your "truth."

Knowledge is available to you from faith. You can "know" what you believe and in what you believe, because it is validated by your experience and your hope. Knowledge is also available to you from facts. You can "know" that a book is a book. But these are two different ways of "knowing," not to be confused with each other. Neither are they at war with each other. They are simply based on two different kinds of knowledge.

Throughout this book, I will be including personal stories in the attempt to model the process of faith-building. These stories are not presented as self-glorification or self-negation, but as illustrations of one person's struggle to arrive at personal faith with a passion. They are what I "know." I hope you will be inspired to express your personal stories.

INTRODUCTION:
HOW TO BUILD YOUR SPIRITUAL HOUSE OF FAITH

Everyone needs a spiritual house of faith. You build your house out of "belief bricks" to withstand the winds and rain during the tough times of life. You make your own belief bricks out of "clay" and "straw." (See my book, *The Three Little Pigs Revisited*, Pair'o'Docs Press, 2002.)

The clay is what you already have in your heart and soul, your unconscious and unprocessed faith. Clay consists of spiritual experiences of your life, some good and some bad, including moments when you felt the presence or absence of God. The problem is that you haven't thought through these experiences to find the meaning in them. Without reflection, these experiences languish in your unconscious, but have a profound impact on your spiritual life. Most people operate out of their clay in their daily activities, so we could follow each other around for forty-eight hours and then describe the other's unconscious faith.

The straw is religious information that you bring into your spiritual life through your mental processes. Straw is what you are told about faith, what you read or view or study concerning spiritual matters. This is material in your consciousness, coming to you from others in speeches, lessons, sermons, Bible, books, movies, television shows, or conversations with friends.

To make a belief brick, you have to take in straw and find if and where it touches your clay. If it does, you know it instinctively. You feel it resonate with your spirit. If the straw doesn't touch you, you put it aside or throw it away. The straw you put aside and store away may become clay when it is forgotten and becomes a part of the unconscious. When it touches, you have to reflect on your experience to see what's behind the connection, carefully mixing straw with clay and molding it into a brick. Then you imprint your initials in the brick, claiming it as your own, and bake it until it's hard. You put that belief brick in its place in your house of faith and start on the next brick.

Many people believe only what they have been given by others, including many church people whose only statement of faith is a creed they have memorized or a collection of slogans they have heard over and over. Theirs is a secondhand faith. Their spiritual lives stagnate or die because they put too much emphasis on straw. They try to force themselves to believe what other people say. But it is what they have experienced, their clay, that causes them to believe or disbelieve to the depths of their spirits. Unfortunately, when the winds of adversity blow strongly, their houses blow away, leaving them nothing to believe.

Other people have rebelled so totally against all the religious "straw" stuffed down their throats that they won't believe anything but what they experience themselves. These people don't take the word of anyone else on anything spiritual. Feeling totally self-reliant, they refuse to consider input from outside themselves, including the Bible, so they build their houses exclusively with the clay of their experiences. But they lose something, too. They are like travelers who set out on a long journey without a willingness to read a map. Thousands of others have journeyed toward the same destinations and left records of their travels, but these fiercely independent people refuse to use anything that has been discovered before. Unfortunately, when the rains of tragedy pour down, their houses of clay melt away, exposing their spiritual nakedness.

If you put forth the effort to build your spiritual house with belief bricks, you will have a structure that stands the test of time. Then, you may want to remodel and renovate from time to time, throwing away old bricks, making new bricks and adding new rooms. This will be uniquely your own house of faith, made up of your bricks, which will serve you well.

> **Paul of Tarsus was the most successful salesperson of the early Jesus movement.** The faith of his childhood, adolescence, and early adulthood was Pharisaical Judaism. His most esteemed rabbi was the wise Gamaliel of Jerusalem, a leader of the more progressive Hillel faction of the Pharisees. Nevertheless, Paul acted like he was closer to the stricter, more conservative Shammai faction of the Pharisees.
>
> After his experience of the "risen and glorified" Jesus on the road to Damascus, he found it necessary to go off to Arabia by himself for three years and build his own faith. There, he threw away many beliefs he had held to be precious. He revised other articles of faith he had been taught. Most importantly for Christianity, he formed many new belief bricks to use in building his new house of faith.
>
> The conscious expression of his personal faith became a very significant section of the New Testament. Paul's personal faith is considered by many as the "inerrant word of God." Paul developed his own faith in his own unique way, reflecting his life experiences. His expressed beliefs about Jesus, for example, were directly related to his experience on the Damascus road. Because he took the time to do this necessary task, he developed a passionate belief that Jesus was the Messiah and the Savior of all who would believe in his lordship. **He was completely willing to become a martyr for that.**

Many of the early Church fathers constructed their theology with bricks made of clay of their experience combined with the testimony of witnesses and the writings of Paul.

> **Augustine was the Bishop of Hippo in north Africa around 400 CE.** In his adolescence and young adulthood, he lived a pagan life he later described as "sinful" and "debauched." He had a concubine for 14 years. She gave

birth to a son who soon proved to be brilliant. The son died at age 18. The boy's death decimated Augustine. A book by Cicero, the celebrated Roman statesman, orator and writer, started him on his quest for wisdom and a fulfilling life.

He joined an heretical Christian group first, because it gave him the answer to the problem of evil, a problem he wrestled with the rest of his life because of his early experiences, his clay. Influenced by the distinguished Christian preacher, Ambrose, in Milan, Italy, he acknowledged himself to be a slave to sexual desire and lust of wealth. In the midst of a deep sense of guilt, he experienced the grace of God, along with God's forgiveness and love. Putting together the straw from Ambrose with his own clay, Augustine proceeded to make his bricks and build his spiritual house of faith. The written expression of his faith continues to have an enormous effect on religious orthodoxy.

This book does not encourage a "do-it-yourself" religion-building. This is about empowering you to discover your spiritual experiences and unconscious faith, and then teaching you how to tie that into the rich spiritual traditions available. This book encourages you to think creatively, but it does not intend to give you a license for spiritual insanity, so you can justify encouraging your followers to drink cyanide-laced Koolaid or jump their souls on a passing comet.

Section A of this book takes you into your experiences (clay) for a little "theo-therapy." Section B explores religious information (straw) that passed through your eyes and ears a long time ago and has become invisible. Section C walks you through some important religious information (straw) in a format in which you have choices to make. Section D teaches how to make belief bricks and bring integrity to your personal faith.

If you build your personal faith and stop there, you miss the point. "Bringing personal faith to conscious expression" means expressing your spirituality in who you are, in what you say, and in what you do, including what you create. The last section of the book, Section E, is concerned with how you live out of your house of faith on a daily basis in the real world.

SECTION A

MASSAGING YOUR CLAY
TO UNDERSTAND YOUR SPIRITUAL EXPERIENCES

Make a list of the most graphic memories you carry around with you all the time, pictures of the most dramatic and traumatic events of your life, beginning as far back as you can remember. This is your spiritual photo album. These are mental photographs of the most vivid events, the most important moments, the best and worst moments, the most dynamic incidences you have ever experienced. You remember these moments so well that you know what people were wearing, what time of day it was, or where certain persons were standing or sitting. On the next page you will find space for you to make this list of mental photographs.

After you have jotted down a few descriptive notes about each picture, look carefully at them to determine whether there is evidence of the presence or absence of God in any or all of these events. Most of these pictures are a part of your clay, because the deeper meaning of these events has yet to be determined.

> At a recent "Personal Faith with a Passion" workshop, I asked the participants to make notes about the most vivid pictures they carry around in their minds. Everyone was writing quietly when I noticed that Henry, a tall, burly guy sitting at the back of the room, had tears streaming down his face. I moved closer to ask what the trouble was.
>
> "Ray, three of the most vivid pictures I carry around in my head break my heart," he said softly. "In the first picture, I am holding my oldest son in my arms as he dies of heart failure. In the second picture, I am holding my second son in my arms as he dies of cancer. In the third picture, I am watching my youngest son being unloaded from a plane on a stretcher. He was returning from a honeymoon trip to Mexico when his plane crashed. My son's bride was killed and he was crippled for life."
>
> I then asked the question that brought Henry to the workshop: "Where was God in those pictures?"
>
> "God wasn't there," answered Henry.

DESCRIPTIONS OF THE PICTURES
IN YOUR SPIRITUAL PHOTOGRAPH ALBUM
THE MOST GRAPHIC MEMORIES
BURNED INTO YOUR BRAIN IN STILL LIFE

1.

2.

3.

4.

5.

6.

7.

8.

9.

10.

11.

12.

CHAPTER 1
IN WHOSE FACE HAVE YOU SEEN THE FACE OF GOD?

Look in your clay, your life experiences, to find when and where you have experienced the presence of God. Look through your spiritual photo album for pictures which include the presence of God. For many of us, particularly for the extroverts among us, the most common way we experience God is through encounters and relationships with people.

In your younger years and throughout your life, you have experienced qualities in other people that, at that point in time, you felt or thought were God-like. Experiences involving people in your early life were especially powerful in forming your ideas about God. Sometimes these experiences and the qualities exhibited by these people told you good things about God. Sometimes they told you bad things. Only you know which ones were burned most deeply into your brain. Some people hate God because the God they've seen in others is so bad that they can't believe God could be anything but bad. Some people love God because the God they've seen in others loved them, affirmed them and accepted them. Here are a few scenarios.

What are the names of those people who have loved you or now love you unconditionally? "Unconditionally" means that they loved/love you as you were/are, with all your strengths and with all your weaknesses. There is nothing you have to improve on before they can love you more. Their love is not conditioned on a demand for you to be or become what they want you to be or become. Their unconditional love for you does not require them to approve or even like everything you do. But they have accepted and treasured you as a human being. You may have experienced God in and through people who have loved you unconditionally.

Who are the people who taught you the most important stuff you know? In the broad definition of education, formal and informal, you have had many educators. Some are professionals. Others are family members, friends, peers, and even total strangers. Some of them gave you information. Others gave you ideas, insights and direction. A part of the answer to the question above has to do with what you consider to be the "most important stuff you know." "Stuff" may include a lot of categories, like relationship stuff or work stuff or financial stuff or spiritual stuff. You may have experienced God as a teacher in and through those people who have taught you.

My major professor at Vanderbilt University Divinity School was Dr. Philip Hyatt. Dr. Hyatt was a well-known and world-renowned scholar of the Hebrew Bible. He had studied and written so much on the prophet Jeremiah that it was rumored he knew Jeremiah personally. In the late 60's, he was nearing retirement and was in poor health, so he had a cot in his office and at two o'clock every afternoon, he took an hour's nap. While I made a habit of calling the members of the faculty by their first names, it was always "Dr. Hyatt." I didn't feel comfortable calling God by his first name, and I was convinced that God took a two o'clock nap every day.

What are the names of people who have shown you a life lived in the presence of God? These are saints, men and women who are godly in their lives. Their spirituality is exhibited in the way they conduct themselves in relationships, with kindness, gentleness, compassion and humility. They give and receive love generously, living life today as if there were no tomorrow. You may have seen the face of God in the faces of these saints.

Near Sparta, Tennessee, lived a man named Eston Myers, a saint. He came in my office one day and told me about two times he had died. He had known not one but two near death experiences (NDEs). He had severe heart disease. His first death occurred during an open-heart surgery that went wrong. He flat-lined and the surgery team did all they knew to do, to no avail. He was aware of all they were doing and heard everything they said, but he was having "that peaceful, easy feeling" and seeing the bright light. The only nurse still around the table was peeling off the last electrical impulse wire when the monitor gave off a beep, indicating heart activity. She gave a shout for the team to come back, while Eston silently screamed for them to leave him alone.

This experience and another like it removed all fear from Eston's spirit. He knew that every day could be his last, so he lived as though there were no tomorrow. His priorities were absolutely in order. He overcame heavy chest pain every waking moment without complaint to demonstrate kindness, gentleness, compassion and humility. He lived his life in the presence of God.

Who disciplined you in your childhood and youth? Who told you what was right and wrong and rewarded you for doing right and punished you for doing wrong? They may have spanked your bottom or patted you on the head. They may have given gifts or withheld privileges. Discipline is a specialized form of education and a subcategory of teaching, but a teacher and one who disciplines are not always one and the same. Chances are, if you have a significant person who disciplined you in your background, you probably have a feeling that God rewards you for good deeds and punishes you for the bad things you do. That was a dominant concept in ancient Hebrew religion and is prevalent in Christianity today.

Has anyone abused you, physically, emotionally or sexually? The statistics provide shocking evidence that many in our society have been deliberately abused, especially females. This kind of abuse is based on the lust for power and control, with the stronger controlling the weaker, the older controlling the younger, and occasionally the younger controlling the older, if the older is the weaker. When you are a child, a powerful abuser may appear like a bad God to you. In your clay, that may cause you to assume that you are not worthy of God's love, only God's abuse.

A woman I had never met before came into my office and told me she needed to resolve her hatred toward her father. She was in her late twenties and her father had died recently. He had abused her every way he could. He had beat her with his fists. He had called her every vile name imaginable. He had raped her repeatedly. She had nothing to believe in and she hated God because she heard that God was like your father.

I suggested that we do role-playing therapy and she could tell her father whatever she wanted to tell him now, things she didn't tell him while he was alive. I suggested that she pretend I was her father, but she said, "No, Dr. Dykes, I couldn't do that." So I suggested the empty-seat scenario and she stood and began talking to her dead father, slowly at first. Gradually, the tempo and volume grew until, in a veritable rage, she cursed him a blue streak and consigned his soul to the depths of Hell. Completely spent, she collapsed in her seat. After minutes of silence, she said, "It's over," and got up and thanked me and walked out. I never saw her again.

Who are the people who controlled your decision-making in your late teens or early adulthood? In the time in your life when you were trying to learn the true meaning of freedom and responsibility, these people were still trying to dictate who you were and what you were to do, your identity and your actions. The issue here is the freedom or bondage of the human will. Some people like external control and some do not. Either way, you may have viewed control as a God-like quality. If so, God would be manifested as either a benevolent despot or an intruder on personal space.

What are the names of those who have functioned as authority figures in your workplace? These people supervised your work, evaluated your performance, and were responsible for the amount of your paycheck. They may have been friends or enemies. They may have known what they were doing or not. They may have known what you were supposed to do or not. They may have led by example or only talked a good game. But they were "The Boss" and that demanded your complete loyalty. To the extent that you now see God as "The Boss" or the "Big Man Upstairs," these people may have supplied the images you see when you think of God.

At the Coca-Cola syrup plant in Atlanta, Georgia, where I worked for three summers when I was fresh out of college, the assistant plant superintendent was "Squeaky." His high-pitched voice got him his moniker, along with the fact that he could cuss like a sailor. I learned to cuss from Squeaky. He had such incredibly intricate combinations of cuss words. We all started the work day with nice clean uniforms, white with green pinstripe, but by day's end we had sweat, dirt and syrup covering us from head to toe, and Squeaky was as nasty as the rest of us. He was "The Boss" and fifty years old, but he could work rings around us twenty-somethings. He had our complete loyalty and if he had told us to march backwards to Chattanooga, we would have done it. Squeaky was a leader, and we young guns admired him.

Has anybody ever rescued you from a dangerous, frightening or life-threatening situation or literally saved your life? It's easy to see how such a person could be seen as a God image. It may have been a law enforcement officer, a firefighter, an emergency medical technician, a physician, or a lifeguard, for example. If you have experienced that, it would be logical that God as a rescuer would have an important place in your clay.

Then there are your heroes and heroines, people you have known personally and perhaps idolized. They function or functioned as your role models in areas like sports, marriage, and vocational choice. They mean a great deal to you because you want or wanted to be like them. You owe a lot of your present identity to them. Your heroes, heroines and role models define your personality to a great extent. Are your role models images of God for you?

I cannot overemphasize the important role that people play and have played in the experiences of God in your life. It is no wonder that most people understand God in anthropomorphic terms, God in human form.

> In the middle of Edinburgh, Scotland, lies the Queen's Park, next to Holyrood Palace. In the middle of the park sits a worn-down, extinct volcano, in the shape of a reclining lion. The top of the lion's head is called Arthur's Seat. It's a great sledding hill because few trees grow on it, and there is not much other vegetation either.
>
> Alex and I were classmates. He lived on the west side of the park and I lived on the east side. One particular day after school, we grabbed our sleds, met in the middle of the park, and sledded until dark. We finished on the west side, so we went to Alex's flat for tea, then I caught the bus home.
>
> When I walked in the back door, there was dinner on the table, but no family. No one answered upstairs, so I opened the front door and found my mother and sister standing outside. "Where have you been? When did you get here? Do you know what time it is? Why didn't you call?" all preceded the news flash, "Your father is out there in the park, looking for you."
>
> When the questions and answers were finished, I could hear Daddy tramping through the snow on that moonless night and calling for me. All my life, Daddy has called me "Man," and that night he was shouting at the top of his lungs, "Man, where are you? Man, can you hear me? Man, are you hurt? Man, answer me!"

I waited until he stopped shouting to catch his breath, and then I yelled out, "Daddy, I'm home! I'm home!" I could hear him gasp, then say "O my God," and then he began to run, crunching along toward the park gate. I ran down the icy road from the house to the park gate to meet him.

There, under a canopy of brightly shining stars, we ran into each other's arms and hugged for all we were worth. Daddy didn't fuss at me. He didn't punish me. He didn't even ask me questions. He just said, "Man, I was afraid I had lost you. I was afraid you were hurt or even dead in the snow, unable to come home, and I had to find you and bring you home. I thank God you're OK. Let's go home."

That loving hug felt good that night. Several years later, the meaning of the experience came clear and it saved my spiritual life. After battling for years with the concept of the judging and punishing God, whom I could never satisfy, I fired that God and experienced spiritual death. In the depths of hell, I remembered that snowy night and a father who loved me so much that he would look for me in the cold, all night if necessary, until he found me. I began putting together the concept of a God who is a Perfect Parent, loving me as I am, accepting me for who I am, not waiting to love me until I achieve perfection. Daddy had modeled such a loving God for me that starry, starry night.

I. IN WHOSE FACE HAVE YOU SEEN THE FACE OF GOD?

In your younger years and throughout your life, you have experienced God-like qualities in people with whom you interacted. In the following categories, list the names of people you know who exhibited these qualities any time in your life.

Those who have loved you unconditionally, accepting you as you were, expecting no change

Those who taught you the most important stuff you know

Those who showed you a life lived in the presence of God

Those who disciplined you in your childhood and youth

Those who abused you, physically, emotionally, or sexually

Those who controlled your decision-making in your late teens or adulthood

Those who functioned as authority figures in the workplace

Those who rescued you from a frightening or life-threatening situation

Those who were your real-life heroes or heroines, people you have known personally

Those who were your personal role models in sports, marriage, vocational choice

Choose two people you have listed and write briefly what those persons' contributions were to your life, one positively and one negatively.

CHAPTER 2

WHERE HAVE YOU EXPERIENCED GOD IN NATURE AND LIFE EVENTS?

Throughout your life, you have experienced God in nature and events of life, outstanding experiences when you felt the presence or absence of God. However, you couldn't or didn't make any belief bricks at the time, so the experiences became a part of your clay. You may have been a child when they happened, too immature to draw lasting meaning from them. You may not have had any straw to mix with the clay, any reference point to help you understand the experience. But these were important times which you need to reflect on to draw out the meaning of the experiences and the impact they have had on your spirit.

This chapter is about remembering your experiences of nature and life events and massaging your clay. It's a nostalgia trip. It's a touch of "theo-therapy" as opposed to psychotherapy. Look for the spiritual in obvious and odd places and times. What pictures do you see?

Have you ever experienced God in the dawn of a new day? Do you ever get up and actually watch the sun rise?

> **We have a real Easter sunrise service in Oklahoma City. There are about fifteen of us on the bank of Lake Hefner, usually in the cold and the wind, to watch the sun rise. And we celebrate "spiritual resurrection." It's great! If the elements cooperate, the sunrise is gorgeous, splendid and wonderful. We really feel the presence of God in a powerful way as we celebrate a God who has made provision for the rebirth and re-creation of every human being in his or her lifetime and the re-creation of every new day.**

Perhaps nothing draws more oohs and aahs than a beautiful sunset. The marvelous array of colors, the shapes of clouds, the calmness of dusk all contribute to the moment of worship and reflection in which you may have experienced the presence of God. Sunrises and sunsets sometimes lead to spiritual awakenings.

Have you ever experienced God in an absolutely awesome view?

> **Have you ever been to the north rim of the Grand Canyon? If you have, you know what I mean. The north rim is a state park. You go out there, and you walk along the top of a little outcropping on a narrow path. You stand there, and you feel like you're in the middle of the canyon on this outcropping. What I observed was that even the children are quiet. It's like they know they're in the middle of a holy place, and they are whispering to one another. They're happy, but they are whispering.**
>
> **And when you go down this narrow path and you meet somebody coming the other direction, it's, "After you."**

"No, after you." You stand there for 5 minutes before somebody goes first. Everybody is so polite. Everybody is so loving. They feel the presence of God there. This is a cathedral of nature. I hope you have had that same experience somewhere in the world.

Have you ever experienced the presence of God in the actions of a beloved pet? Sometimes you can feel God's love in the unconditional love of a pet who is always so happy to see you, who licks your face and lets you know that you are a special human being. Many single people depend on their pets to be their primary companions. There are so many people in our world today whose pets are their only contact with a living thing on a daily basis. That companionship and acceptance is the way many people experience God.

Have you ever experienced God in a dying time? Have you ever held the hand of a loved one when he or she breathed his or her last breath and died peacefully? In the midst of your grief, there may have been a comforting feeling. You may have felt a hug from God in the hug given to you by someone who really cared. In a dying time you may also have felt God's absence.

I experienced the absence of God in the death of our boxer dog, Rocky Fellow. I loved him. I trained him to do several tricks. We were pals. He developed cancer in his back. One day, when he was thirteen, the cancer cut his spinal cord and his hind legs wouldn't work anymore. A majestic dog was no longer able to function with dignity. He could no longer enjoy respect. He could only be pitied. I had to take him to the vet to be put to sleep. I brought him home in his blanket, buried him in his self-fertilized backyard, planted a dogwood tree on top of him, and wept my eyes out. God wasn't there.

What about the presence of God in a catastrophic event like a tornado or hurricane or flood or fire or explosion? Have you been in one? What did you experience? Did you feel anything about the presence or absence of God in the event?

The bombing of the Murrah Building in Oklahoma City and the terrorist attack on the World Trade Center in New York City caused a great deal of discussion about the presence or absence of God. Survivors and families of survivors spoke of miracles and how God had protected them and their loved ones from harm. They experienced the presence of God. Families and friends of the men, women, and children killed in that horrific blast were asking questions relating to how the will of God could allow such a thing to happen. For the most part, they experienced the absence of God.

Have you ever experienced God at a birth time, at the birth of a child, or the birth of an animal? I'm told that a woman, while stretched forty ways from Sunday in the vaginal birthing process, has a hard time finding anything godly to feel, think or say during that time. At the same time the father of the child may be giddy from excitement in a heavenly moment, or in a dead faint on the floor. The mother may have that heavenly experience after the pain subsides. The miracle of birth and the beginning of life often speak of the presence of God as creator.

Have you ever felt the presence or absence of God in a decision-making process? I mean a biggie, not "What am I going to wear tomorrow."

>**After twenty-four years of pastoral ministry, serving three congregations in Tennessee and Oklahoma, it was time for me to move on. I had done everything I could do to advance the mission and ministry of my last pastorate. My passion had become to provide opportunities for unchurched people to come into the church and learn new ways to bring their personal faith to conscious expression.**
>
>**The first option to be rejected was to seek a pastorate in another church in another city, a church that shared my passion and had more resources and zeal to make it happen. However, my wife, the love of my life, is a professor of Hebrew Bible (Old Testament) at a local university and to move away would, at least, put her teaching career in jeopardy (which she was willing to risk), since teaching positions in her area are as scarce as hen's teeth. Clearly, it would not have been ethical for me to seek the pastorate of another church in Oklahoma City and be in competition with my former church.**
>
>**It appeared to me that the only viable option was to create a new ministry based in Oklahoma City. It would be a major risk, both professionally and financially. After much reading, thinking, consultation with friends, meditation and prayer, the Personal Faith Program was born. It is a program which provides full pastoral services, especially faith counseling, to those households who choose not to be involved in the institutional church; supplemental faith counseling for churched people; and workshops on faith-building for churches throughout the United States.**
>
>**Even though there was initial opposition from the local jurisdiction of my denomination to this program, I felt the presence of God in the decision-making process. I felt "called" by God to this new ministry. It has been a big financial struggle, but the program continues to touch more and more people, giving them the freedom to believe their own beliefs with a passion. God was there.**

I hope you have experienced or will experience the presence of God in love-making. And if you are older and married and you haven't, it's time you did. Love-making is a vital part of the experience of life that God created us to enjoy. We should feel God in the midst of a time of love-making. What could be wrong with acknowledging the presence of God in the moment of a mind-blowing orgasm or climax? Many of us were taught that you weren't supposed to use the words "God" and "sex" in the same sentence. We don't need to leave God out of our sex lives.

Have you ever experienced God in a moment of extraordinary growth? It can be emotional growth, spiritual growth, even physical growth.

> **I was a delegate to an annual meeting of a regional governing body (synod) of the Presbyterian Church. We met in St. Petersburg, Florida. Two people had already been nominated to be the presiding officer (moderator), and I had decided to run against them. I came in second. For the next three days of the meeting, I acted like a spoiled brat who didn't get his way. I raised objections just to be objecting. I threw the body into turmoil over technicalities. After the meeting was over and we were gathering our things to go to the airport, a man, whose name I do not remember, came up to me, and in a very loving and patient tone of voice, said, "Ray, I've been watching you make a horse's ass out of yourself throughout this meeting. You've been playing the game called 'I Win, You Lose.' You have a lot of talent and a lot to offer, and you don't need to play that game ever again."**
>
> **That man spoke the word of God to me and it hit me like a ton of bricks. He was clearly an angel (messenger) of God, delivering the message I needed to hear. In the next five minutes, I did some heavy growing up. I stood transfixed on the same spot because I knew I had just experienced the presence of God and I was standing on holy ground.**

How about in a moment of reward or punishment? I'm intrigued by victorious football coaches and players who say that their team won because God "was smiling" on them today. Their claim is the same as saying that God rewarded them because they prayed more than the other team for victory, because God loves them more than the other team, or because they have been morally superior to the other team. A player kneeling in the end zone to thank God for letting him score a touchdown may be saying that God prevented a cornerback from tackling him at the fifteen yard line. What might the cornerback pray?

Have you ever experienced the presence or absence of God in a worship service? In my 24 years in the church, I experienced God in worship on somewhat rare occasions, but I may have been working at it so hard that I missed God in the process. I have felt "strangely warmed" in baptizing a baby on Christmas Eve, listening to the choir sing a beautiful cantata, watching a child wash his mothers' hands and offer her a blessing on

Maundy Thursday, seeing a father place his hands on his daughter's head and offer her a blessing as she is being ordained a church officer, being told you said something meaningful in your sermon that you didn't remember saying and that wasn't in your notes.

Clyde Cromwell sang tenor in the church choir of First Presbyterian Church in Lebanon, Tennessee. One Sunday in a February worship service, Clyde sang beautifully a solo, entitled "There's a Sweet, Sweet Spirit in This Place." A few weeks later, Clyde died suddenly of a cerebral hemorrhage. We mourned his death and our loss. On Easter Sunday, the talented woman who created the chancel floral arrangement outdid herself. She had one large solitary stone positioned on the flower stand with a solitary lily attached to the back, appearing to grow out of the stone. At the offertory, the organist chose to play "There's a Sweet, Sweet Spirit in This Place" and while she was playing, a solitary cricket lodged in that solitary lily growing out of that solitary stone began singing and we were all undone. We experienced not only the presence of Clyde, but also the presence of God with us.

It is helpful to reflect on these experiences of God in nature and life events in a thorough fashion, reflecting on what they have meant to your life and faith, positively and negatively. This is your clay and it is very important. Look carefully for signs of the presence of God in nature and life events every day. They are there!

When I was a six-year-old, we lived in the big house the Baptist church in Tylertown, Mississippi, made available to its pastor. It sat right next door to the church building and just across the street from the elementary school. I remember great big rooms, open windows, an attic fan, and one big bathroom with a four-legged bathtub.

One night my mother told me to get in the bathtub, take my bath quickly, dry off, get on my pajamas and get in bed, since it was way past my bedtime. I got in the bathtub and began to play joyfully in the soapy water with my rubber ducky. Suddenly, out of nowhere but within the bathroom, I heard a very loud "NO!" I looked around and saw that I was alone in the bathroom. My quick childhood deduction was that I had just heard the voice of God telling me NOT to disobey my mother. I moved soap at lightning speed, rinsed off in one motion, pulled out the stopper, toweled off for ten seconds, jumped into pajamas, and ran and crawled under the bed, scared to death of God.

I lived for years after that in fear of God, who watched my every move, even when I was in the bathtub. My fear

was that God would verbally correct me again if I ever disobeyed my mother, so I concentrated on being the very obedient son. I even went for years without stepping on a crack in the sidewalk, because of the old proverb, "Step on a crack, break your mother's back."

There was immediate reaction to this traumatic event, but it was years later before there was reflection on the experience. Then, it became apparent that the probability was that a neighbor was walking his dog, which strayed into the flowerbed under the window of the bathroom, and the man was telling the dog to get out of the flowerbed. But that doesn't change what I experienced that night, nor what it did to my unconscious faith.

Without reflection, I believed God to be "the all-seeing eye watching me," the God to be feared, the God who shouted "NO" at a little boy when he didn't do what his mother told him to do. Upon reflection years later, I rejected that concept of God and threw away the clay which had controlled my thoughts and actions for a long time.

How important it is to reflect on the "God experiences" of your childhood and youth and adulthood. Then you can determine the impact they had on your unconscious faith. Then you can decide whether to use that clay to make bricks with which to build your house of faith today.

2. WHERE HAVE YOU EXPERIENCED GOD IN NATURE AND LIFE EVENTS?

Throughout your life you have experienced God in nature and/or in events of life. In the following categories, list the outstanding experiences in your life when you felt the presence or absence of God, as you understood God at those times.

A beautiful sunrise or sunset

An absolutely awesome view

The experience of a beloved pet

A dying time of a human or an animal

In a catastrophic natural event like a tornado

A birth time of a child or an animal

In a decision-making process

In a time of love-making

In a time of extraordinary growth, either mental, psychological or spiritual

In a moment of reward or punishment

In a worship service

Choose two of the items you have listed and write briefly what these experiences meant to your life and faith, positively and/or negatively.

CHAPTER 3

WHICH STORIES ABOUT GOD-LIKE CHARACTERS TOLD YOU ABOUT GOD?

All your life you look for God-like figures to tell you who you are and how to act. Role models tell you what life is about. They reassure you that the world is just and safe, or they convince you that it is vicious and horrible. Some of these figures are real and others are fiction. If they are people you admire greatly, you unconsciously attribute to them what you think are God-like qualities.

In this chapter, you will move deeper into understanding what you really believe about God as you see how stories have influenced people's concepts of God. This chapter will help you understand what you hope for in your concept of God and what you most desperately yearn for God to be like. You are invited to think of the characters who are your heroes and heroines in every kind of story you have seen or heard and the qualities each of these characters displays.

Stories are so critically important in determining what you believe, and you have lots of them in your memory. I have included several personal stories in this book to model the importance of remembering, identifying and interpreting your faith stories. You have stories that are tucked away, deep within your brain, and they can function as mirrors to your spirit. These stories also have something to do with what you consider to be God-like qualities. What pictures in your spiritual photo album are taken from the variety of stories you have heard and/or seen?

In the story of Cinderella, who is the most God-like character? Is it the fairy godmother or the handsome prince? That depends on what were God-like qualities when you first heard the story.

What are the God-like qualities in the fairy godmother? The fairy godmother is kind, loving, compassionate and giving. She hears Cinderella's prayers and feels her pain. She can transform a young woman, mice and a pumpkin into what they have never been. She does all this with a magic wand. She is helpful. She makes things better. The fairy godmother gives Cinderella what she needs. And she is a SHAZAM god, magic wand and all.

Why is the handsome prince a God-like character? He makes her feel safe and wanted because he accepts her. When she flees at midnight and he loses her, he begins a relentless pursuit to bring her back into his circle of love. He searches for her and when he finds her, he loves her for who she is.

Both characters have God-like qualities. The one you choose today or the one you chose years ago as the more God-like says a great deal about your clay, your unconscious faith. Where did that choice come from?

> *The Poseidon Adventure* is a movie released about 25 years ago. It's about a cruise ship that is turned upside down by a huge wave, a tsunami, and is slowly sinking. The passengers and crew are all trying to get to the bottom of the ship, which is now the highest point and the only section

where there's still air to breathe. They're going up the main propeller shaft, and they're getting close to the top, almost there. And what happens? They run into the last of many obstacles. There's a jet of scalding steam going across their path. The little band of survivors can't get through that.

When the Episcopal minister figures out that there is a gate valve which controls the steam jet, he jumps over there, catches on that gate valve and stops the steam. But now, he can't get back to the propeller shaft. So, he eventually loses his grip and falls to his doom, and the last of the survivors can make it through to their rescue, to the strains of "There Has to Be a Morning After." And there you have a picture of sacrifice as a God-like quality.

In the literature of the human race, in movies and on television, there are stories of heroes, heroines and God-like persons. Some of the stories are biography and some are fiction. When you read them or saw them, they presented to you individuals you admire greatly even today. Bible stories, fables, children's stories, comics or animation, novels, history or biographies: they're all possibilities for places to discover persons or groups of people that exemplify God-like qualities, as you have defined God-like qualities at any point in your experience. What are the stories that have influenced you the most?

Secondly, who are your heroes or heroines in these stories? These individuals manifest personal qualities that you consider to be wonderful. These should be people you don't know personally. The point is to look at what is significant to you about these people, and how that relates to your concept of God.

Thirdly, what are the qualities that each displays? For example, if you were to name the movie, *The Prince of Egypt*, a person would be Moses, and the qualities would be faith or leadership. These are possible God-like qualities of Moses.

A well-known biblical story illustrates what this book is all about. It's about a man who came to understand what he really believed and the impact that had on him. It's the story of Jacob and Esau.

Jacob, or Ya'akov, means in Hebrew, "He who follows close behind but wants to jump in front." Jacob and his twin brother, Esau, whose name means "Redneck" in Hebrew and who was the older by a minute or two, were opposites, very much opposite.

Esau was the redneck. He loved to hunt, fish, play football, things like that. He was into the athletic stuff and outdoor stuff, and he drove a Ford pickup truck with a gun rack in the back window. He had red hair, which was very unusual. He was Daddy Isaac's boy.

Jacob liked to hang around the tent. He liked to cook. He enjoyed playing the piano. He wasn't a physical weakling. He just preferred to hang around with Mom. He was Mommy's boy. His mother's name was Rebekah, which in Hebrew literally means "Tied Tightly in a Stall." I take this to mean that she was a rambunctious woman.

Jacob eventually cheated Esau out of his inheritance as the first-born and also out of his blessing. We may not fully understand this custom of blessing nor its impact, because we haven't experienced it. We do know about inheriting, however. But in ancient times the blessing of the father to the first-born was as big as the inheritance.

Jacob cheated Esau out of both inheritance and blessing. It took Esau a while to figure out that he'd been cheated, but when he did, he said, "I'm gonna kill that boy." And he easily could have.

Word got to Jacob about this, so he "cut a chogey," which means he left town in a hurry, heading north where his mother's brother lived. He married his two first cousins, Leah (which in Hebrew means "heifer") and Rachel (Hebrew for "ewe lamb"). His father-in-law, Laban (Hebrew for "paleface"), tricked him into marrying Leah, when he only wanted to marry Rachel. Later, he got to marry Rachel, picked up at least two good concubines, Bilhah and Zilpah, and they all had a big family with at least thirteen children who are named in the Bible. Then, he cheated his father-in-law out of a lot of sheep, goats, donkeys and camels. But, he got caught by his brothers-in law, and he had to "cut a chogey" again.

He had to go back down south, because there was nowhere else to go. Now, he had his brother down south, who said he was going to kill him the next time he saw him. His father-in-law was chasing him from the north. Jacob and Laban got together and squared up on everything, but he couldn't go back north. And his brother was coming to meet him with four hundred fighting men.

How many fighting men did Jacob have? Zero. He had herdsmen. He had wives and concubines, and he had children. He had sheep, goats, camels, and donkeys, but he didn't have any fighting men, and here came Esau with four hundred fighting men.

Jacob confronted his physical mortality in a significant manner. He could see them setting up his tombstone any moment now. And so, the night before he and his brother were to have their public meeting, at which time he was going to die, the twins got together for a little man-to-man, one-on-one, mano a mano, hand-to-hand combat, a wrestling match.

If you read the story carefully, you can see that Jacob's concept of God in his early years was that God was big, mean and stupid, just like he thought of Esau. So he got together that night beside the stream called Jabbok (which means "emptied out" in Hebrew) with his concept of God. Jacob wrestled with his concept of God, personified in his brother. (God personified is an "angel" in the Hebrew Bible.)

And he wrestled with his concept until the day was about to break. Meanwhile, Esau had knocked Jacob's hip out of joint. And Jacob was doing a leg ride. (A leg ride in wrestling is where you just hang on, buying time, while the other person drags you around the mat.)

Finally, Esau said, "Let go of me. The sun's about to come up."

Jacob said, "I won't let you go 'til you bless me!"

Esau said, "What's your name? (That's an interesting question, isn't it?) What's your name, Boy?"

He was forced to say, "My name is 'He Who Follows Close Behind but Wants to Jump in Front.'"

And his brother said to him, "Your name will no longer be 'He Who Follows Close Behind but Wants to Jump in Front.' Your name from this day on will be 'Israel' or 'He Who Wrestles With God,' (that's what "Israel" means in Hebrew) because you have wrestled with your concept of God tonight, and you have reached a new place in your life and your faith." Esau left hurriedly so no one would see them together.

Next morning at the public meeting with his brother, "Dead Man" Jacob went crawling on his belly toward his brother. His brother had four hundred fighting men standing behind him. Esau was standing twenty yards away, and Jacob was crawling toward him and toward his death, trying to save his children.

Then, something happened, something so rare that is only recorded three or four times in the Bible. Esau ran to his brother! In the Middle East, a chief of a tribe never ran, because he wore a full-length robe and for him to show his ankles was a disgrace. He couldn't have disgraced himself more if he had stripped naked. Esau disgraced himself in front of four hundred fighting men. They would never let him forget that the rest of his life. They wouldn't joke with him about it. It would be a matter of great disdain.

Beyond just running to his brother, he picked him up out of the dirt and hugged him and kissed him, and they wept together. What was Jacob's response? He said, "In your face, my brother, I see the face of God." And Jacob named that place "Peniel," (which means "Face of God") because he said "I have seen the Face of God" (Genesis 33:11).

What happened there that day to Jacob/Israel? He got a new concept of God. What's that new concept? Instead of God being big, mean, and stupid, God is now loving, forgiving, accepting, caring, willing to disgrace himself even to show love for a brother. That's a very different concept of God than the one he started with the night before.

But what had happened in the meantime? He had acquired a new name. In Hebrew and in Greek, "name" means your total identity. It means who you are. It describes your personality or some distinguishing feature. It's no fluke that his name was "He Who Follows Close Behind but Wants to Jump in Front." That described his personality to a tee. He took advantage of everybody he could. Neither was it a fluke that Esau's name was "Redneck," because that described him to a tee. All those names supposedly described people perfectly. That's why they had those names. It was their identity.

Jacob's identity was changed to Israel. He wasn't who he used to be. At the same time, his concept of God changed. Why did it change? Because he had a new experience of God. He processed that new clay, mixed it with straw from religious information he had received before, and he made a whole ton of new bricks.

Lash LaRue was one of my childhood heroes. Lash LaRue was a cowboy, and he had a bullwhip as his primary weapon. He was deadly accurate with his whip, so accurate that he could whip guns out of the bad guys' hands before they could shoot. Lash was sort of a non-violent cowboy in that he would use his bullwhip instead of his gun whenever he could. We used to go on Saturday mornings to Red Bank Theater in north Chattanooga for nine cents and watch the Lash LaRue serials.

When I was pastor at Central Presbyterian Church in Oklahoma City, the congregation was coming out of the sanctuary one Sunday morning, and I was greeting them at the door. An older man with longish white hair, a visitor I didn't know, shook my hand and said, "God bless you!" and walked on out. The man right behind him said, "Ray, that man was Lash LaRue."

I left the line. I went chasing after him with my pulpit robe flapping in the breeze, all the way out to the parking lot.

And I said, "Mister LaRue, can I have your autograph?" One of my treasured possessions today is my picture of Lash, with the hand-written inscription, "Best wishes from another servant of God, Lash LaRue."

So, things may have happened with the stories that you knew as a child that continue to make an impact on you. You may have re-encountered your stories while raising your children and reading to them. Look at these stories, examine them in light of new experiences and process and re-process them to gain fresh interpretations.

If and when you hear a sermon preached on a Sunday morning, what do you remember best? It's the stories. You know that and the preacher knows that. You remember the stories. So dig into your stories and look for your experiences of God. Look for the God images there, for the characters with God-like qualities. Are there characters in your stories which show up in your spiritual photo album?

I did this exercise in a retreat with a group of middle school students, twelve-, thirteen- and fourteen-year-olds. It was one of the most marvelous experiences that I've had in my life. They were thinking about movies that they'd seen recently. They could click off, "Oh, there's a God-like quality!" "Yeah! Yeah! In that movie, Yeah!" When we got through with this section, they all said, "We'll never go to the movies again without looking for God in the storyline."

That's what you can do. You can look for the symbols. Where are the God-like qualities as you look at the stories you remember? You've got lots of stories that you've heard or read stored in your head. Process the clay of those stories and relate them to your understanding of the nature of God.

3. WHICH STORIES ABOUT GOD-LIKE CHARACTERS TOLD YOU ABOUT GOD?

In the literature of the human race, in movies and on television, there are stories of gods, heroes, and God-like persons. Some of the stories are biography and some are fiction, but they present individuals you admire greatly. These individuals manifest personal qualities that are wonderful to you. In the spaces below, list the stories that presented these persons to you. More importantly, list the persons, historical or fictional, who are your heroes or heroines in these stories, and the qualities each displays. (These should be people you do not know personally.)

Biblical stories, other than stories of Jesus (those will come later)

Fables (like Aesop's fables) or fairy tales (like Cinderella)

Children's stories (like Dr. Seuss)

Comics or animation (like Superman or Sesame Street)

Movies and TV specials

Novels

Histories or biographies

Look at the qualities embodied by these heroes or heroines, and relate them to your understanding of the nature of God at various times in your life.

CHAPTER 4

HOW DO YOU PRAY AND WHAT DO YOU SAY WHEN YOU PRAY?

Prayer has a remarkable and distinctive place in the spiritual lives of most people and communities of faith. Prayer may be among the most personal and, at the same time, the most confused aspects of your relationship with God. You may have a great deal of unprocessed clay about prayer deep down inside.

It is important to look at and understand the position of body parts in prayer, what the various positions mean, and where they came from. There is a social and historical background that can give insights to this matter, and that may help you sort through some difficult issues related to prayer. I'm calling that "how do you pray."

In addition to the way you pray, you may need to deal with the content of your prayers, for example, what you ask God for and what that means about your concept of God. Answers or non-answers to prayer are often at the heart of one's experience of God. Knowing what you believe God can do or will do or ought to do is of critical importance for people who pray. I'm calling that "what you say when you pray."

This chapter is absolutely pivotal to your personal faith development because your ideas about and your practice of prayer hold the key to your unconscious faith, especially what you believe about the nature of God. Massaging your prayer clay will reveal much to you about yourself and your God and your relationship with God.

> I came out of Sunday night worship a little early from First Baptist Church of Clinton, Mississippi, home of my alma mater, Mississippi College. At the bottom of the stairs I saw my psychology professor, Donald Clark, looking back up at the church building and shaking his head. He said, "Ray, when Russell McIntire called on Deacon Brown to lead the closing prayer, the first thing the deacon said was, 'Let us play, I mean, pray.' I've heard many other people make that mistake, and it just occurred to me that it's a Freudian slip. He was right the first time. He was 'playing' at praying."

It occurred to me that night that I had played at praying as long as I could remember. Four years later while in Divinity School, I did a careful study of the theology of prayer and found that precious little had been written in an objective fashion about prayer. Paul Tillich's book, *The New Being*, contained a chapter on "The Paradox of Prayer" and that was very helpful.

I discovered I was still praying to a concept of God I had already left behind. I had to learn new ways to pray to the new concept of God that had been revealed to me.

Prayer is a mirror of one's concept of God. How you pray should have integrity with your concept of God. Your belief about God should be truthfully exhibited in the way you pray and what you say when you pray. If you are struggling to know what you believe about God, look at the way you pray and what you say or think in prayer. After you have worked out your conscious concept of God, you will have to determine the best way to mirror that concept and pray to God with integrity.

In the Middle East, when Muslims pray to Allah, they kneel down on a rug or cloth and put their foreheads on the ground, because that's the way you humble yourself before an oriental monarch. It is appropriate to perform an act that shows humility and contrition before someone with the power of life and death over you. The Bible speaks of "fear" toward God, but the word really implies "worship" or "reverence" and the Middle Eastern way to show reverence is to bow to the ground.

Anglicans and Episcopalians kneel when they pray, because that's the way you show respect for the English king. The English kneel before the sovereign in ceremonial tribute, even though the western monarch doesn't have the power of life and death.

Scottish Presbyterians do not kneel, but sit to pray, because the Scottish people didn't like the English king. Before King James VI of Scotland became James I of England, the Scots had as little to do with the English king as they could, except when they went to battle with the English. After the royal Stewart family lost control of the English throne, the same sentiment prevailed.

Two little Scottish boys: one was Episcopalian; one was Church of Scotland (Presbyterian). Scots refer to Episcopalians as "Piscies." This little Presbyterian boy said to the Episcopalian kid, "Piscie, Piscie, says 'amen' down on his knees and up again!"

The Episcopalian boy replied, "Presby, Presby, cannot bend, says his prayers on his hinter end."

Forms of prayer have historical reasons. Holding your open hands against one another is an accepted custom of prayer, because the word "prayer" comes from the French word *prière*, which means "to beg." And if you have your hands together, the next move is to bring them down in front of you and open them slightly on the top side to receive something.

You bow your head and close your eyes when you pray, primarily because that's the custom. That's what you do in deference to the monarch. To the extent that you see God as the king, that is appropriate. If, however, you don't see God as the king, you don't have to do that. A lot of people say they close their eyes when they pray because they can concentrate better. That's just fine. But if you can concentrate better with your eyes open, then pray with your eyes open.

Most of what you do when you pray is cultural and historical, not theological. But, what about the words of prayer, what you say when you pray?

What does it mean about your concept of God when, while praying, you ask God to do things for you and give things to you? This is a **prayer of petition**. What if those things are material things, like cars, houses, jobs, or people, like spouses? What if you ask God to do things for you and give things to you of a material nature? What does that mean about your concept of God? Is God like Santa Claus? If that's what you believe, the first step is to recognize your belief. The second step is to admit that God is like Santa Claus, fulfilling your wish list. The third step is to decide whether you want to keep or change this concept of God. The fourth step is to work toward making the content of your prayers reflect your personal faith.

What if you ask God to do things for you and give things to you that aren't material? Then, you believe that God is the source of those great intangible gifts that you need. So, you're asking for them. "Ask and you'll receive. Seek and you'll find. Knock and the door will be opened"(Matthew 7:7). This is still a prayer of petition. The things you ask for are different. You may be seeking to incorporate into your life what you understand to be God-like qualities, like love, peace of mind, calmness of spirit, patience, compassion, joy, and wisdom.

What does it mean about your concept of God when you ask God to do things for others and give things to others? This is called **intercessory prayer**. What's your concept of God when you say, "God, my son needs a new job. Can you handle that?" Is God the powerful provider? You've got to have that concept of power if you're going to pray that way. When you ask for material gifts, you are assuming God has power. You're also assuming God can hear you and will respond.

What if Dick and Marilyn have an identical physical problem, and you pray for Dick but you don't pray for Marilyn, and Dick gets over it and Marilyn doesn't? What are you assuming about God? Does it means that God plays favorites with people with physical problems? Many prayers like this are verbalized, where unconsciously the concept of God in that prayer is that God is a discriminatory God.

I've started doing something new any time I pray an intercessory prayer. I let the person know that I'm praying for him or her, one way or another. I say personally, "Mike, I'm praying for you." I call him on the phone and say, "Roy, I'm praying for you." I send her a note which says, "Helen, I just prayed for you and I want you to know that." I send Rachel an e-mail which reads, "Rachel, I'm praying for you today."

This makes a prayer of intercession more powerful. If I don't let them know I'm praying for them, am I practicing voodoo? I wonder about that. Do I count on that prayer to bounce off an orbiting God and hit the recipient with whatever I prayed for?

> We were having some work done in the church, and an electrician was working in the building. He wasn't a member of the church, just an electrician from Ace Electrical Company. This guy had been in the church for two weeks, running wires for heating and air conditioning controls. He came in my office the last day he was there and said, "Ray, I've walked by your office door a lot during these two weeks. You know, I've seen you praying with and for a lot of people. A lot of the members of your congregation have come, and I've seen you take them by the hand. But I haven't seen anybody come in here and pray for you." He said, "Would you come over on this side of the desk, please, and sit down and let me pray for you?"
>
> I came over and sat in the chair, and the guy took my hand and prayed for me. That was the first time in 20 years in the ministry that anybody had ever come in my office and taken my hand and prayed for me. And, I felt the presence of God in that electrician's prayer and care for me.

I told that story in a sermon shortly after it happened. Florence Little came into my office every week for the rest of her life and prayed for me. She did that 'til she died. If you are a church person, have you ever gone into your pastor's office and taken his or her hand and prayed for him or her?

Very popular at the beginning of worship services is a **prayer of confession**. The worship leader states quite clearly that you are supposed to confess your sins to God in an attitude of prayer and often gives the congregation a written prayer to read. With some people there is confusion about how a prayer read by a whole congregation has anything to do with the individual. What does praying a prayer of confession say about your concept of God? Does this mean God wants to know about your sins and needs you to spill the beans? Does God appreciate your confession even though God already knows what you have done wrong? Does God forgive your sins? What additional assumptions about the nature of God are behind a prayer of confession?

Prayers of thanksgiving are prayed in many different settings: at the supper table, in a church worship service, on a walk in the woods in the spring, after recovering from the twenty-four hour flu, and in hundreds of other situations. These are prayers thanking God for what God has placed at your disposal, done for you and given to you and to others. The assumption that informs most prayers of thanksgiving is that God is a good, giving God who provides for you and those you love. How does that fit with you?

A prayer of acceptance is a new and exciting way to pray. What does it mean about your concept of God when, while praying, you let God know that you are taking the gifts that God has already given you?

> **I have this mental picture of ten million tons of the love of God sitting at my left elbow. It was put there when I was born. I have to reach and take it and put it in my chest. Sometimes when I'm driving, I will sit at a red light and say, "God, I am taking your love! I am taking your love."**
>
> **I'm one of those verbal people. So, I have to say this out loud. One day, I was feeling unloved, and I went in the living room and sat in my Lazy-Boy and leaned back. I sat there and I was reaching, literally, and taking and pushing in the love of God, and I was starting to feel good. It was getting better every time I reached and put more love in my heart! But my phone started ringing in my office. I thought, "I'll let the answering machine get it!" while I load in some more of God's love. But then I thought, "Dadgummit, I'd better answer that." So I jumped up and ran into the office, snatched up the phone before I had a chance to look at the caller ID, and said, "Ray Dykes speaking!"**
>
> **The young woman said, "I'm sorry. I have the wrong number," and she hung up.**

Then I looked at the caller ID. It gives first name last and last name first. It said, "Love, Valerie." A stranger named Valerie Love had misdialed while I was receiving the love of God. If I had asked for a sign, I had one.

I'm convinced that the great intangible gifts of God are sitting right here next to us. They've already been given to us. If they've already been given to us, is it insulting for us to ask God for them again? Is it insulting for us to ask God for what God has already placed at our disposal in an amount that we can never possibly utilize? This is like saying, "Here, Helen. This dollar bill is yours!"

And Helen says to me, "Hey, Ray. Would you give me a dollar bill?"

"Well, Helen, I've already given you a dollar bill! Pick it up!"

What are the great intangible gifts of God that are already placed at your disposal? In addition to love, you may have peace of mind, calmness of spirit, patience, wisdom, mercy, grace, and a number of other intangible gifts of God. You don't manufacture a single one of these. All these come from God and are placed at your disposal, because God wants you to have every one of them in full measure.

Do you know why you sometimes have a bad day? Because you forget to take what's sitting at your left elbow. Is the act of accepting these gifts a prayer? Do you want to know how to make life good today and tonight and tomorrow? Grab the great intangible gifts of God, tell God "thank you," and pass these gifts on to the people around you. This is some straw about prayer for you.

Has God ever told you exactly the words to use when you pray? Christians were given a model prayer, the "Lord's Prayer." Does that mean that you're always supposed to say those exact words? Does God tell you when you're supposed to pray? Paul says to pray without ceasing, because that relates to living your life in communication and communion with God. That's a **living prayer**. Is anything you do unknown to God? Do you communicate everything you do? If everything you do is communicated with God, do you like your prayer?

Another part of the question is: do you think of prayer as one-way or two-way? Either way is okay. If you like prayer to be two-way, that's fine. This usually means, "I talk to God and God talks back to me. I feel God's presence so strongly when I pray, I believe God is talking back, answering my prayer." Others think of prayer as one-way, based on the definition from the French word *prière*, "to beg." You communicate to God in prayer rather than with God, and God communicates to you in revelation rather than with you. You can say that when God speaks to you, it's revelation rather than answer to prayer.

Another issue is whether God answers prayer or God's revelation comes to you on God's time, terms and agenda. Do you define God's answer to prayer as telling God what to answer and when to answer? Do you think it is appropriate to bark out orders to God like a sergeant barks out orders to a private?

The bottom line is the definition. What's your definition of prayer? It's important for you to spend some time coming up with your definition of prayer. How important is prayer in your life? How much does your prayer life tell you about your concept of

God? The way that you pray and what you say when you pray should inform you about what you believe about God. Likewise, what you believe about God should tell you how to pray and what to say when you pray. When you pull these things together, you have integrity.

A bishop was sailing on a ship in the Caribbean 150 years ago, and the ship had a problem and they had to go into port for a day to fix it. But the bishop was determined that he wasn't going to waste that day. So, he walked down the beach, and he came upon three local fishermen. He began a conversation with them, and they spoke pigeon English. He told them he was a bishop and asked them, "Do you know what Christian is? I'm a Christian bishop."

The fishermen said, "Oh, we Christian, we Christian!"

The Bishop said, "Well, how did that happen?"

They answered, "Oh, missionary come to island long time ago, teach us about Jesus. We Christian."

He said, "That's wonderful. When you pray, how do you pray?"

"Ah," they said, "When we pray, we say, 'We are three, you are three. Have mercy on us.'"

Well, the bishop was shocked. This was heretical prayer. And he said, "Do you mean nobody taught you the Lord's Prayer?"

"No. We don't know Lord's Prayer."

So he spent the rest of the day, teaching them the Lord's Prayer. Little by little they learned it. And he was gratified that by the end of the day they could all say the Lord's Prayer perfectly. He then got on his boat the next morning and sailed away, feeling very righteous about this.

Several months later, his ship was passing by this same island. In the evening, he was standing out on the deck, saying his prayers, looking over toward that island, thinking what a great joy and pleasure it had been to be able to teach the Lord's Prayer to the three ignorant fishermen.

As he looked toward the island, he saw three lights coming toward his ship. He watched the lights get brighter and closer. As he kept watching he began to make out three figures running across the sea, coming toward the boat. By this time, other people had noticed. The captain stopped the ship, as these three men came running across the water right up to the side of the ship. They stopped next to the ship and the bishop stood at the rail. He looked down and recognized the three fishermen he had met before, and in awe said, "What can I do for you?"

The three fishermen said, "Oh, Bishop. We hear you come close to island. We hurry, hurry meet you."

"What can I do for you?" he repeated humbly.

"Oh, Bishop, we forget pretty prayer you taught us. Would you teach us prayer again?"

The bishop in total awe and humility said, "Go back to your homes, and when you pray, say, "We are three. You are three. Have mercy on us."

(Adapted from *The Spirituality of Imperfection* by Kurtz and Ketcham, Bantam Books, 1994, who adapted it from The *Song of the Bird* by Anthony de Mello, Doubleday-Image, 1982.)

Learning what you believe about prayer can be the beginning of knowing what you believe about the nature of God. It was for me.

"Likewise the Spirit helps us in our weakness; for we do not know how to pray as we ought, but that very Spirit intercedes with sighs too deep for words" (Romans 8:26).

The Spirit's intercession for us "with sighs too deep for words" is a vague and certainly a mystical statement by Paul. Paul may have felt words were useless when one communicates with God out of one's innermost being. In such intimacy when words of prayer fail us, perhaps God knows and hears our hearts.

What has been your practice in prayer? How do you pray and what do you say when you pray? Why? Have you found anything in your clay about prayer?

4. HOW DO YOU PRAY AND WHAT DO YOU SAY WHEN YOU PRAY?

What does it mean about your concept of God, when, while praying, you:
Bow your head? Look up?

Close your eyes? Keep your eyes open?

Kneel? Sit down?

Put your hands together? Raise your arms and hands?

Speak words? Think thoughts?

What does it say about your concept of God when, while praying, you:
Ask God to do things for you and give things to you (petition)?

Ask God to do things for others and give things to others (intercession)?

Confess your sins to God (confession)?

Thank God for what God has done for and given to you and others (thanksgiving)?

Let God know you are taking the gifts God has already given you (acceptance)?

Live your life in communication to God (living)?

Do you think of prayer as one-way or two-way? What is the difference between "God answers prayer" and "God's revelation to you" or "the word of God to you"?

What is your definition of "prayer"?

How important is prayer in your life and faith? How much does your prayer life tell you about your concept of God? What does your concept of God tell you about how you should pray and what you should say or think or do when you pray?

SECTION B

SORTING THROUGH OLD STRAW FOR SPIRITUAL MESSAGES FROM YOUR PAST

It began as "straw," but that was so long ago that it has become "clay." It's in the unconscious because you have forgotten it. You heard it repeatedly and it stuck in there somewhere, but it never was processed. Now it's time to sort through these religious messages and decide whether to work with them to find the meaning or to throw this straw, now clay, as far away as possible.

Religious information infiltrates our minds from a great many sources, and much of what you learn about faith is forgotten. But, much of this forgotten information can continue to inform your unconscious faith. There may be a large reservoir of information that drives you to believe what you believe without your knowing why you believe it. Many people express their faith with memorized words, not knowing what the words mean.

In Section A of this book, you involved yourself in "theo-therapy," digging into your experiences for glimpses of God in people, nature and life events, stories and prayer. I hope you remembered experiences and those mental pictures of critical moments in your life that will be helpful as you make "belief bricks," using this clay to mix with the straw you will be encountering in the next sections.

This is a transition section, illustrating that there is a grey area here. It is not always possible to distinguish between clay and straw, but usually it is clear. The litmus test is this: clay is experience that is unprocessed and residing in the unconscious; straw is religious information that comes into your consciousness.

There are many sources from which you receive religious information. In this section you will be dealing with two prime examples of religious information that you received mentally and may have forgotten, repressed or let sit so long that you are no longer aware that they're there: religious teachings and the words of hymns, psalms and spiritual songs. The question is how much authority you have given them in your faith.

CHAPTER 5
WHO TOLD YOU THAT?

Even if you never went to a seminary, divinity school or graduate school of theology where clergy are trained, you were, nevertheless, probably taught what to believe about religious matters. Somebody gave you the words you use to express what you are supposed to believe. Sometimes you forget who told you what to believe, and you may not have sufficiently considered the source. That can get you in a world of hurt. Or, you may have received words of wisdom that you need to recall to consciousness to use in the brick-making process. That may bless your life.

The subject is religious information and the question is whether there are big chunks of this information in your brain that you have never really and fully evaluated. The purpose of this chapter is to encourage you to dig out this straw that has turned into clay and determine whether this information meshes with your life experience. It is your experience, and only your experience, that can validate this information.

Martha and Jim came to see me for family counseling. This was Martha's second marriage. Martha had been married when she was nineteen to a man who was physically abusive. After five years of beatings, she declared her freedom and got a divorce. That was a major problem for her, since she and her family were members of the Church of Christ, a fundamentalist alliance of churches that do not countenance divorce, unless your spouse is adulterous. A few years after divorcing her first husband, she and Jim were happily married and living away from her home church. They had two children and a wonderful home life.

Then, members of family and church showed up to tell Martha that she was an adulteress, according to the New Testament, living in sin. They crushed on her that if she died tonight, her immortal soul would live all eternity in the depths of hell. Their solution to her problem was to annul her marriage to Jim, let him keep the children, go back to her first husband and submit to his abuse for the rest of her mortal existence. Even after our counseling session, that's precisely what she did, because Martha didn't know what she believed. She simply accepted what others told her without examining what she believed, especially with regard to her own concepts of self-worth, God and family. If she had built her own faith, she may have chosen love and life.

Who were your most influential theology professors? There is a very good chance that your parent or parents told you most of what you believe. There is even a better chance that it was your mother who taught you religious matters in your home, since women are involved in Christian education more than men by a two-to-one margin.

Can you remember the situations in which your mother or father spoke to you of her or his faith or values or spiritual hope? Can you remember the general topics presented or the specific words used? What authority do these words still have for you?

Grandparents are often surrogates for parents in religious education of children. Sometimes, they impart spiritual wisdom to their grandchildren more readily and more easily than the children's parents. Lessons of faith are regularly taught to children sitting on a grandparent's knee. Do you remember sage words of spiritual advice from your grandparents?

Sunday School teachers may have been important sources of information for you if you grew up in the church. Beginning with pre-school class, you probably were taught about the people of the Bible, beginning with Jesus, then Paul and Peter and Mary, then Adam and Eve, Noah, Abraham, Moses, Ruth, David, Esther and a few others. In elementary class, you would have been taught the stories of the Bible, like the creation of the world, the great flood, the Israelite exodus from Egypt, the conquest of Canaan, the birth of Jesus, the death and resurrection of Jesus. In junior high class, you might have been asked to consider biblical concepts, such as sin, justice, love, salvation, heaven and hell, and morality. In senior high class, the subject was the application of biblical principles to daily life in your society. This is a typical structure of Sunday School curriculum in many Christian churches and denominations. If you attended Sunday School, what have you forgotten that you were taught about all this? Who were the notable teachers?

> **I remember my senior high Sunday School teacher at First Baptist Church, Jefferson City, Tennessee. I don't remember anything he taught us, but I remember a contest we had between the girls' class and the boys' class. Whoever lost had to provide a steak dinner for the other class. We had a 100 point system. You got 30 points for studying your lesson, 20 for staying for the worship service, 10 for making a contribution, 20 for just being there, 10 for being on time, and 10 for bringing your Bible. The contest was about how many people showed up, and the 100 point system. We were playing the numbers game in the Baptist church.**
>
> **Sunday School started at 9:30 a.m., and at 9:15 we would call the guys who weren't there to see if they were on the way. If they weren't, we would hop in the teacher's station wagon, and we would go to their house, get 'em out of bed, throw them in the back of the station wagon along with their clothes, and they would get dressed while we drove to the church building. I don't remember what the teacher taught us, but I do remember that contest!**

You may have been influenced by church creeds, confessions, and catechisms as sources of your unconscious faith. During my years as pastor of Presbyterian churches, I found that many Presbyterian laypersons relied upon the Apostles' Creed for the words of their expression of faith. The Apostles' Creed was originally a baptismal creed to be recited by an adolescent or adult at the time of his or her baptism. It was conceived as a personal expression of faith, its recitation necessary to permit one to be baptized. It was written in part to refute the belief of a group of early Christians, called "Docetics," who maintained that Jesus only appeared to die, so it says four ways that Jesus really died physically: ". . . was crucified, dead and buried; he descended into hell." (Most Christians don't know that "he descended into hell" means that Jesus really died, since the "hell" referred to is the place where all dead people go after they die, the underworld under the flat earth.) If you grew up in a creedal church like Presbyterian, Catholic, Episcopal, Methodist, or Lutheran, you were probably exposed to the Apostles' Creed, but have you really thought seriously about the words and concepts in it? Now is the time to dig out a copy and consider the words carefully.

The Nicene Creed was the first creed written to be recited by congregations gathered in worship. It was written in 325 in the town of Nicaea in northwestern Turkey by a group of Christian bishops, called together by the emperor of the Roman Empire, Constantine, to settle the dispute over the nature of Jesus, who and what Jesus was and is, and how Jesus relates to God. The resulting creed was more political than it was theological. Constantine had seen the fussing and fighting taking place among these early Christians about the nature of Jesus, and he demanded a compromise expression of faith on which all Christians could agree. The last section of the creed is on Holy Spirit and wasn't finished until 70 years later. It was left unfinished in 325 because the bishops ran out of time. When it was finished, it was not agreed to by all Christians for centuries and later became one of the principal reasons for the division between the Roman Catholic and Eastern Orthodox Churches.

Again, if you grew up in the church, the Nicene Creed and other creeds may have had a great influence on your unconscious faith. These words and concepts need to be examined to see if their imprint has been stamped on your brain with helpful or hurtful results. Is it important to you to know some of the history of the formation and original intent of the creeds to see what you may have picked up unwittingly along the way?

For church people, the most powerful source of unconscious faith is the sermons preached Sunday after Sunday. They may have been about the love of God or the wrath of God. They may have been about the goodness of God's creation or the wickedness of the "Devil's" domain. They may have made you leave worship feeling fear and guilt or renewal and refreshment. They put many thoughts into your head at the time, some of which have influenced you positively or negatively even though you have never processed those thoughts.

It was Jonathan Edwards who ignited the Great Revival in the original colonies of the young United States of America with his sermon entitled "Sinners in the Hands of an Angry God." The sermon contained a vivid word picture of a spider dangling on a silken thread above a roaring fire, symbolizing an individual in peril of falling into the depths of hell. This one sermon had a powerful impact on those who heard it. Sermons still have an impact, consciously and unconsciously.

Who were the most important preachers in your past? Can you name one or more? What did they say to you about important matters of faith that you remember? What have you repressed into your unconscious? Chances are when you make an important faith statement, it was a preacher who told you that.

Some other important theology professors in your life could have been school teachers, if you attended a parochial school or a private Christian school. If you took a course or courses in religion or philosophy in college, the professor may have "told you that." Some of the words of faith you profess to believe may have reached your intellect through authors of books on spiritual matters. For example, Hermann Hesse in *Siddhartha* and Erich Fromm in *The Art of Loving* wrote words that were pivotal in my faith life years ago.

An important question to ask yourself about any and all of your "theology professors" is whether they were helping you explore your own spirituality or seeking to indoctrinate you. It seems that the world is full of those who, for their own personal reasons, are bent on indoctrination.

Betsy Sellars of Lebanon, Tennessee, dealt with the issue of indoctrination. She said, "This (technique) has offered me justification and allowance for the thoughts I have had since I was a child. I don't call my thoughts 'beliefs' because I 'believed' what I was taught to believe and forced myself to believe because I wanted to be a good Christian."

Twenty-five-year-old Andi McComb wrote, "Instead of blindly accepting as fact what I have been told throughout the years, I am beginning to think and question and make my own decisions as to what to believe. This path of molding bricks and creating a theology is difficult. It is the hardest path to follow. I only hope I can follow it." What you are told by your theological professors may help you or it may hurt you. The important thing is to decide for yourself what you want in your faith and what you choose not to believe. Look carefully at this straw that has turned to clay and choose well.

Somebody taught me a long time ago that when you're having a theological debate with somebody, and you're losing, the two phrases to remember are: "What do you mean by that?" and "Who told you that?" You'll slow them down, anyway.

5. WHO TOLD YOU THAT?

Who taught you your faith? Who gave you the words you use, or have used, to say what you believe? Name your most influential theology professors. Do you remember anything specific they taught you about faith that you still believe?

Parent(s) or Guardian(s)

Sunday School teacher(s)

Preacher(s)/Pastor(s)

Peer(s)

School teacher(s)

College professor(s)

Author(s)

Looking over the above, is there something you believe very strongly that one of these people taught you?

Did any of your professors encourage you to think for yourself about matters of faith? Did any discourage you?

CHAPTER 6

HAVE YOU LOOKED AT THE WORDS OF THE SPIRITUAL SONGS YOU SANG?

Much of the unconscious faith on which church people base their lives comes not from what the preacher says or what the Bible tells them but from the songs they sang in church. I encourage you to examine some songs you have known all your lives and can quote without any trouble at all.

It is a fact that rhyming verse is the easiest literature to memorize. You can recall nursery rhymes easily because of the meter and the sound. Songs from your childhood are more deeply etched in your memory than yesterday's lunch menu. Yet, a close look at these verses may cause considerable discomfort. For example, how does it make you feel when you sing "Amazing grace . . . that saved a **wretch** like me"? or "Would he devote that sacred head for such a **worm** as I?"

To begin with, think of five of your favorite hymns and spiritual songs. Many mainline Christians and evangelicals will be surprised to learn that much of what has penetrated their hearts most deeply was put there by a blind songwriter, Fanny Jane Crosby, who wrote thousands of hymn texts in the last half of the nineteenth century, including "To God Be the Glory" and "Jesus, Keep Me Near the Cross."

It is estimated that we learn more from what we sing than from any other source. If that's true, the hymns and spiritual songs may have contributed mightily to your theology consciously or unconsciously, especially if you grew up in the church. Did you know that many hymns in the Methodist hymn book were written by John and Charles Wesley, the founders of Methodism, and that a great deal of Methodist theology is from their hymn book?

> **I grew up a little Baptist boy, and I was singing the song, "Alas and did my savior bleed and did my sovereign die? Would he devote that sacred head for such a worm as I?" I grew up feeling that, in the eyes of God, I was a worm. Unprocessed, in my clay, I was a worm.**
>
> **"Amazing grace, how sweet the sound that saved a wretch like me." That was in my clay. I finally had to wrestle with it, and I had to say, "I'm NOT a wretch in the sight of God." But until that time, I believed that, and I was a worm and a wretch in my own eyes.**
>
> **As a result of that, I tried to be perfect. I was Mr. Southern Baptist Convention of 1963. I was perfect. I was morally perfect, because it was so important that I prove to God that I was not a worm or a wretch. That had a traumatic and demoralizing effect on me as I struggled with my self-concept and my concept of God.**

Look at the most important words, phrases or themes in your five favorite hymns or songs. How are those words, phrases or themes present in your theology? Have you really addressed them? Have you really dealt with those words? "A Mighty Fortress Is Our God"? "Immortal, Invisible, God Only Wise"? Do you really believe that? "Immortal, Invisible, God Only Wise"? Many revivalist spiritual songs tell of the blood of Jesus on the cross, speaking of the crimson flood, and a fountain filled with blood drawn from Immanuel's veins. Do those songs fit in with your concept of Jesus? Why or why not?

Do you know where this idea of flowing blood came from? At the time of Jesus and the early Christian church, the Greco-Roman world embraced many Greek mystery religions. For purposes of baptism, one of these religions made use of a *taurabolium* to baptize those who wished to join their cult. A *taurabolium* was a pit dug in the earth. A grate was placed over the top of the pit. Wearing white robes, those being initiated were placed down under the grate where they would stand while the members of the cult brought a bull and killed it on the grate. They would then cut the bull and let it bleed on the people down below. Consequently, those joining the cult were washed in the blood of the bull, signifying their acceptance of the cult's belief system through participation in the initiation process.

In the story of the crucifixion of Jesus, there wasn't anybody standing under the cross, getting bloodied by Jesus' blood. Yet, this image of blood baptism comes from the *taurabolia* concept in the Greek mystery religions and is picked up and carried through by the Letter to the Hebrews in the New Testament. But it got into our songs. From our songs, it got into our hearts and minds, and we haven't examined it. It's just lying there, unexamined! What are we going to do with it?

Not only do hymns reflect an understanding of who Jesus was, but they also reflect the particular faith orientation of congregations as a whole. There are "first person churches," "second person churches," and "third person churches," speaking of the three persons of the Trinity. Some churches are "first person" because the hymns and songs the members sing are primarily about God, the Father, the Creator, hymns like "Holy, Holy, Holy, Lord God Almighty." "Second person churches" sing most often about Jesus, the second person of the Trinity, songs like "What a Friend We Have in Jesus." Pentecostal churches are "third person churches." They sing a majority of the time about Holy Spirit, with songs like "Holy Spirit, Breathe on Me."

The theological emphasis of the church may have helped you or scarred you. These hymns and songs could do either one. They could lift you up or take you down. You have to look and see what they've done to you, what they've done for you as straw that may have become clay by this point in your life.

In the earliest days, before people even wrote, poets give us literature in song and poetic form. The oldest written piece in the Bible is Miriam's song in Exodus 15:21, the earliest form of which was oral, and it was passed on orally for centuries before it was written:

> Sing to the Lord, for He has triumphed gloriously;
> Horse and rider, he has thrown into the sea.

It's poetry. Why do you remember poetry? Because it rhymes and has meter. Why do you remember songs? Because they have rhyme and meter. These things stick in your clay. They are straw when they go in, and you remember them. But then you forget them and they pass into your unconscious. Unless you examine them, they could be hurting you. They hurt me with this "worm" and "wretch" business, until I brought it to consciousness, examined it and thought about it. On the other hand, the straw of songs and hymns may be helping you in your faith development with phrases like " . . . God's re-creation of the new day." Either way, bring them to consciousness to help you recognize and verbalize what you believe.

Hymn writers and spiritual song writers have brought their personal faith to conscious expression. You may have sung their faith, which is straw to you, without thinking about the words you were singing. Singing a song repeatedly stores it in your memory in an unprocessed form, making it a part of your unconscious faith, i.e. your clay. The challenge is to process this strategic material consciously and deal with this straw which turned into clay.

6. HAVE YOU LOOKED AT THE WORDS OF THE SPIRITUAL SONGS YOU SANG?

It is estimated that we learn more from what we sing than from all other sources. If that is true, then hymns and spiritual songs may have contributed mightily to your theology, consciously or unconsciously, especially if you grew up in the church.

List five (5) of your favorite hymns and spiritual songs
1.
2.
3.
4.
5.

What are the most important words, phrases, or themes of these five hymns or songs?

How are those words, phrases, or themes included in your present theology?

Does it mean anything to you that "Amazing Grace" does not mention Jesus once?

What does it mean to you when the first line of "Amazing Grace" speaks of "a wretch like me"?

Many "revivalist" spiritual songs tell of the blood of Jesus on the cross, speaking of the "crimson flood" and the "fountain filled with blood drawn from Emmanuel's veins." Do these songs fit in with your concept of Jesus? Why or why not?

Many images of God are present in the great hymns of the church, such as "Holy, Holy, Holy, Lord God Almighty" and "Immortal, Invisible, God Only Wise" and "A Mighty Fortress." Were these or any other images helpful to you in the construction of your concept of God? Which ones? Why?

SECTION C

GATHERING NEW STRAW FROM CURRENT SPIRITUAL MESSAGES

Religious teachings are often presented as all-or-nothing propositions. Either you believe them or you don't. If you believe them, you're in. If you don't, you're out. In contrast, in this section I examine some of the most controversial teachings of the Jewish and Christian traditions and point out that there are belief options and what some of the options are.

One of the quickest ways to find out about God is to listen to what others say about God. This is gathering new straw. One of the most important things to know about straw is that you are under no obligation to believe the advertising of the people who put it out. All sorts of people label their straw the only true straw. They say God made their straw and only their straw. My message is "Don't waste your time trying to convince them otherwise. If the straw they advertise doesn't connect with your clay, let it go."

> The nature instructor at the summer boys' camp kept a collection of live snakes: black snakes, king snakes, chicken snakes, rattlesnakes, copperheads. All were common snakes and they behaved predictably. The boys fed them, and the snakes ate. Then one week the instructor purchased a beautiful brown coachwhip snake and added it to the collection. After a few weeks, the snake began to look lifeless. The instructor and the boys decided it must be hungry.
>
> So they got a wiener. Two boys held the snake while the instructor shoved the wiener down its throat. Then he slowly massaged the hot dog down the snake's body to where he figured its stomach must be. They were so proud of their good deed, but it was such a small wiener and such a big snake. So, they repeated the process with a second wiener. Then, feeling righteous, they put the snake back in its cage and went to bed.
>
> The next morning, they found that beautiful coachwhip snake as dead as a doornail. They killed that snake giving it what they decided it needed. They killed that snake by feeding it food its body couldn't digest in a way its body couldn't handle.

That snake is like a lot of people who have been force-fed by religious zealots and religious institutions that decided what those people needed and proceeded to cram it down their throats. Those doing the cramming came off feeling righteous. Those having it crammed down their throats sometimes got their faith destroyed.

You need to learn how to throw away what you don't believe, that stuff others have given you that doesn't work for you. However, to ignore the wisdom passed down during 3,000 years of religious searching would cut you off from some pretty good ideas about who God is and how you might get to know God. It is necessary to explore this wisdom and reflect on what you discover. This section helps you break down and examine what you have been taught about some of the most important aspects of Jewish and Christian faiths. Some chapters of this section will be important for you only if you come from a Christian church background.

CHAPTER 7
DOES THE BIBLE HAVE ERRORS AND CONTRADICTIONS AND WHAT DIFFERENCE DOES IT MAKE?

What you believe about the inspiration and authority of the Bible can have a massive impact on what you believe in many other areas of faith. The Bible has effected billions of people in very positive ways as the best-selling book of all time, but it has caused divisions in modern Christianity over the question of whether there are errors in its pages.

There are issues and questions to confront about the Bible. Many people engage in bibliolatry, worshiping the Bible as a God, complete with its own little shrine on the coffee table. Many others count on the Bible to be the one present and tangible manifestation of God in their world, the "Word of God." However, relatively few people read the Bible enough to become knowledgeable of its contents, choosing instead to let others tell them what it says.

There are contradictions in the Bible. The details of a few of the errors and contradictions in the Bible are presented below. I find that its errors and contradictions make it more credible rather than less. A contradiction indicates that one thing may be right and one may be wrong, or both may be wrong, but both cannot be right. Therefore, it is fair to classify a contradiction as an **error** on the part of someone, probably an ancient editor. Contradictions in two of the creation stories and in the two stories of Noah and the Flood are outlined. The accounts of two New Testament locations of the ascension of Jesus are listed. Other errors and contradictions from the Hebrew Bible and the New Testament make it clear that this issue must not be brushed aside.

Here is a listing of some of the contradictions in the Bible, beginning with the most blatant and obvious:

1. I Samuel 17:50-51 says that David killed Goliath. II Samuel 21:19 says that Elhanan killed the same Goliath. Elhanan is not David's middle name. Goliath didn't die twice.
2. Matthew 28:2 and Mark 16:5 say there was one "angel" or "young man" at the empty tomb on Easter morning. Luke 24:4 says there were "two men."
3. In Matthew 28:7 and Mark 16:7, the women are told to tell the disciples to go to Galilee where they will see the resurrected Christ. In Luke 24, Jesus appears to the disciples in Jerusalem and ascends to heaven from Bethany, which is just outside Jerusalem, whereas in Matthew 28, Jesus commissions the disciples on a mountain in Galilee.
4. In the first two chapters in the Bible are found two contradictory accounts of creation. There are at least eight points of contrast between the accounts:

Old Creation Story in Genesis 2

   a. The story comes from the southern storyteller, an "Uncle Remus" of this and other stories.
   b. It was first written about 1000 BCE.
   c. The pre-creation situation is dry desert because that's what you find in southern Israel.

d. Creation of humanity precedes the creation of vegetation and animal life.
   e. Man and woman, Adam and Eve, are created in two separate acts.
   f. The Creator is called "the Lord God" (Yahweh Elohim).
   g. Creation is a hands-on experience for the Lord God.
   h. One important aspect of the concept of the Lord God presented in this story is fertility.

New Creation Story in Genesis 1

   a. This is the religious establishment's official, authorized **description** of creation.
   b. This description was first written about 500 BCE, in or around the time the Jews returned to Jerusalem from exile in Babylon. It has a Babylonian flavor to it.
   c. The pre-creation situation is watery chaos because Babylon was located between the Tigris and Euphrates Rivers.
   d. Order of creation is light, sky, sea, earth, vegetation, sun and moon and stars, birds, sea creatures, land animals, and lastly, humanity.
   e. Creation of humanity is a single act.
   f. The Creator is called "God" (Elohim).
   g. The Creator is present only through the commands that cause the creative acts to occur.
   h. One important aspect of the concept of God presented in this description is bringing order out of chaos.

5. In Genesis 6-8, there are two stories of the Great Flood, a common story in the literature of the Middle East. These stories have been intermingled in the text by the editors/redactors. The older of the stories is found in Genesis 6:8-10; 7:1-10,16c; 8:6-12,20-22. This story comes from 1000 BCE and may have Egyptian influence. The newer story, found in Genesis 6:9-22; 7:11-24; 8:1-5,13-19; 9:1-17, comes from 500 BCE with Babylonian influence. Here are six contradictions:

Old Flood Story
(Genesis 6:8-10; 7:1-10,16c; 8:6-12,20-22)

   a. Human wickedness prompts "YHWH" (the Lord) to wipe out descendants of Adam, along with animals, reptiles and birds, but not sea creatures.
   b. No details are given about the size of the ark or what it's made from or how it's made.
   c. Noah is instructed to take seven (7) pairs of edible animals on board, and one pair of animals that you don't eat.
   d. The flood is a simple matter of too much rain falling for "forty days and forty nights," a Hebrew idiomatic phrase meaning "long enough" or "a very long time."
   e. The ark lands in an unknown location after Noah sends out a dove on three occasions to test for dry ground. All passengers disembark soon after, it seems.
   f. Noah initiates a covenant-making ceremony with YHWH. He builds an altar, kills one of every edible specie of animal and bird and cooks the meat on the altar. YHWH is pleased and promises never again to destroy every living thing.

New Flood Story
(Genesis 6:9-22; 7:11-24; 8:1-5,13-19; 9:1-17)

a. "God" decides to kill everything under the heavens in which there is the "spirit of God," in response to humans' filling the Earth with violence.
b. Details are given of the size and shape of the ark, along with specific directions as to how it is to be built and from what it is to be made.
c. Noah is instructed to take **one** pair of all animals on board and is reminded to take food for all.
d. The flood is a complex matter involving the undoing of creation. The dome that divided the waters above the Earth from the waters below the Earth is severely threatened when water comes down from above and comes up from below for 150 days.
e. The ark comes to rest in the mountains of Upper Mesopotamia and Noah and his family and all the animals remain in the ark for several months before disembarking.
f. God initiates a covenant-making ceremony with Noah. He gives the humans similar instructions to those he gave to the humans in the description of creation in the first chapter of Genesis. God gives the rainbow as a sign of his promise that he will never again drown every living thing.

You don't have to believe everything in the Bible is literally true to have a solid faith. But if you want to talk about your faith with other people, you better know where you stand on Scripture. This is one of the most contentious matters in the Christian faith right now. It has ripped entire denominations asunder. It is the centerpiece of many religious discussions.

We have been hammered with the teaching that the Bible is the supreme authority of the Christian faith. It has been said over and again that the Bible is the "proof of the faith." It proves that what we believe is true, as long as we don't tinker with it. There is security and certainty in the Bible, as long as we trust every word in its "original" Elizabethan English meaning. However, throughout the centuries, the Bible has evoked some fierce battles over its authority.

You may have been told that you have to believe every single word is without error, because the Bible is like a house of cards. If one card is removed from the bottom of the stack, the whole house falls. To keep the whole house standing, the Bible must be taken literally. However, does taking the words literally mean that we practice it literally? No one has yet been found who practices everything or attempts to practice everything that the Bible says, even among those who believe that the Bible is without error. There are those who attempt to live out certain biblical teachings, and it is very much a matter of choice which teachings one follows. Whole churches and denominations have been founded by groups who decided to focus on certain teachings. Every Christian, therefore, has his or her chosen teachings, while other teachings are deliberately omitted or unwittingly ignored.

Several decades ago, there was a survey done in the Presbyterian Church about what members, elders, and pastors believed about the authority of scripture. What came out of that was basically four viewpoints.

1. Some people believe that every word written in the Bible was literally dictated by God to the individuals who wrote it down on paper. Since God, in essence, wrote the Bible, it's the divine word of God. Since God doesn't make mistakes, the Bible is without error in all matters, including history, geography, and science.
2. Some people believe that the writers of the Bible wrote down what they believed to be the truth about God and the faith stories of the people of God. These writers were inspired by God as they wrote, so the Bible is the true word of God. However, they were influenced by their cultural contexts, so the scientific and historical data may be more symbolic than literal.
3. Some people believe that the Bible is a collection of faith stories and faith statements, which were never intended to be taken as more than that. Certainly, there are errors in the historical, geographical and scientific data presented in the Bible. But the basic truths about God and life and love contained in the Bible make it a very important book, if not THE most important book.
4. Lastly, there are some people who believe that the Bible, especially the New Testament, was written to convince people to come to a particular point of view and that various accounts do not have much basis in fact at all. They believe that the accounts of the life of Jesus are particularly suspect because they were written to convince the Greco-Roman world that Jesus was the "Son of God" and the Messiah or Christ, promised to the Jews.

What do you believe about the inspiration and authority of the Bible? You need to decide where you are on the spectrum. Lots of people will try to shame those who pick a view different from theirs. The point is to know what you believe.

My testimony to you is that I love the Bible. I've been studying the Bible on a professional basis since 1966. I've done translations and paraphrases of sections of it. The Bible is my book, but I don't worship it. When my Bible wears out, do you know what I do with it? I drop it in the trash can. Get another one. It's not holy! The God that it talks about is holy. It's not an icon that I put on my coffee table with a candle beside it and bow down to it. I write all over my Bibles, and you can, too. I love the Bible so much that I'm willing to let it be what it is instead of trying to make it into something it isn't.

It's far more important for the Bible to read me than for me to read the Bible. In other words, when I'm reading the Bible and I find a passage in there where I say, "Ah ha! Been there, done that!" the Bible just read me. The trick is to find yourself in the book. Discovering the biblical characters'

> experiences and emotions which parallel your own makes the Bible relevant for you. Otherwise, the Bible remains dusty old stories about people living two or three millennia ago. When you identify, when you read the Bible and find your biography in there, then you're getting into the Bible! If you read it, and it's about somebody else, that doesn't matter to you a whole lot. But when you find yourself in there, then you're reading the Bible.

As a result, inspiration is very evident in the reader when you read the Bible and make an effort to understand its historical and contemporary meaning. It's definitely inspiring when you find yourself in the experience of someone whose story is told in the Bible and allow the straw of that story to connect with your clay. If all the inspiration in the world happened on the writing end, but you never find anything in there that applies to you, does it matter? The Bible is possibly the most important straw that you're going to deal with. Let the Bible read you! Give it a chance! You're going to have to open it, ask questions of the text, and let the text read you.

Most of the Bible is hard to read. We all need help in reading and studying it. Almost every time I read a passage, I see something I never saw before. And I've been working on it professionally for a long time. There's so much there! You'll never wear it out.

> **Just recently I saw something new in the story of Moses, in a section telling about a battle between the Israelites and the Amalekites in the wilderness of southern Israel (Exodus 17:8-13). Moses went up on a hill and held his hands up while the battle raged. As long as his hands were up, the Israelites were winning. But when his hands came down, Aaron and Hur held up his hands for him. The name of that hill is "Rephidim," which means "Reclining Couches" in Hebrew. It may have been named that because those two guys rolled some rocks up and made a Lazy-Boy structure out of them. They sat Moses on that construction and made armrests to prop up his elbows. I'd never thought about that before.**

The Hebrew storytellers had a great sense of humor, by the way. And there's a great deal of humor in the Bible that's never been translated because the translators thought it might be too embarrassing.

You may not have been taught that much of the Bible was written to be understood symbolically and not literally. If the Bible were a wondrous and beautiful flower garden, the literal reader picks the flowers and enjoys them until they die, while the symbolic reader views them in their natural context and enjoys them as they change, forever.

Why do so many do such violence to the Bible for the sake of their own safety and security? Let the Bible be what it was intended to be, a book of wonder-filled God symbols.

The Bible is read by a very small percentage of those who claim to be Christians. It is studied by even less. The vast majority of Christians is illiterate about the Bible. It says "Holy Bible" on the outside and we don't want to be sacrilegious and read anything that's holy. Besides, it's very old. Then there are those who boast of how many times they have read the Bible from cover to cover. The Bible is worshiped as an idol by some Christians and ignored by most.

It can be risky to confuse the Bible with God. The Bible is a vehicle through which the divine-human encounter can and does take place. This has to do with distinguishing the reality and that which witnesses to or symbolizes the reality. It really does not matter whether the story of the prodigal son ever happened. The story points beyond itself to a profound reality that God's arms are open, and there is nothing standing between God and you. That's good news!

In simple terms, the Bible is the record of God's revelation. It is the story of the activity of God in, among, and for God's people. From time to time, various writers felt a need to write out the stories, events, and happenings of God's people, and these writings eventually became the Bible. The Bible is a book about faith, not a book about facts. The writers were bringing their personal and corporate faith to conscious expression. Since all the writers had not experienced God in the same way, they expressed their ideas differently. These different ideas appear as contradictions in some of the stories. To ask which is right and which is wrong is to miss the point. There are differences in the stories for sure. Does that make the Bible more or less valuable to you?

The Bible is a book of faith, using symbols and words to point beyond itself to God. The Bible is a window through which we might, with spectacles of faith, behold God.

Did any of this straw touch your clay?

7. DOES THE BIBLE HAVE ERRORS AND CONTRADICTIONS, AND WHAT DIFFERENCE DOES IT MAKE?

Some people believe that every word written in the Bible was literally dictated by God to the individuals who wrote it down on paper. Since God, in essence, wrote the Bible, it is the Divine Word of God. Since God doesn't make mistakes, the Bible is without error in all matters, including history, geography, and science.

Do you agree or disagree, and why?

Some people believe that the writers of the Bible wrote down what they believed to be the truths about God and the faith stories of the people of God. These writers were inspired by God as they wrote, so the Bible is the true Word of God. However, they were influenced by their cultural contexts, so the scientific and historical data may be more symbolic than literal.

Do you agree or disagree, and why?

Some believe that the Bible is a collection of faith stories and faith statements, which were never intended to be taken as more than that. Certainly, there are errors in the historical, geographical, and scientific data presented in the Bible, but the basic truths about God and life and love contained therein make the Bible a very important book, if not the most important book.

Do you agree or disagree, and why?

Some believe that the Bible, especially the New Testament, is a propaganda piece, without much basis in fact at all. The accounts of the life of Jesus are particularly suspect, since they were written to convince the Greco-Roman world that Jesus was the "Son of God" and the Messiah/Christ promised to the Jews.

Do you agree or disagree, and why?

CHAPTER 8

ARE THERE PROBLEMS WITH JESUS AS "THE DIVINE SON OF GOD?"

Jesus of Nazareth is the problem of Christianity. Just let that sink in for a minute. Jesus is the problem of Christianity. He's not the problem of Judaism. He's not the problem of Buddhism or Islam or Taoism or Confucianism. He's the problem of Christianity.

Jesus has always been the philosophical and theological problem of Christianity, especially the views of his humanity and divinity. The history of the divine Jesus can be traced back to Persia and Zoroastrianism and the person of Mithras, a divine/human figure sent down to earth by the good god to aid in the fight against the bad god. This concept of the divine savior sent down to earth in human form was picked up by Greek Gnosticism, whose thought world was dominant in the Roman Empire in the first century of the Common Era (CE).

Christianity started as a sect of Judaism. Jesus was the problem. Problem doesn't mean bad. Problem means something you have to work on. The earliest Christian writers, from Paul to Augustine, struggled with the nature of Jesus and his relationship to God. Some wrote that Jesus was not created by God but co-existed with God before the creation of the universe. Others wrote that Jesus was God squeezed into a human form, and in that form God suffered with and for humankind. Another significant group of Christians, the Docetics, taught that Jesus, being totally divine, never experienced human birth. He just showed up one day in Galilee, having snatched a human body off the rack. He only appeared to die on the cross, since no god ever dies. Not many of these people agreed on who Jesus was/is or what Jesus did.

The people of the first century thought in Greek/Gnostic thought forms (to be explained shortly); therefore, most of the New Testament was written in those forms. Jesus had to be presented as divine to compete with the other gods present in the Roman Empire. To have presented him as human would have meant the crib death of Christianity.

Today, most church people profess to believe in both the humanity and divinity of Jesus, but lean toward the divine Jesus. Most unchurched people today appreciate the human Jesus but have serious difficulties, at least, with Jesus as a second god alongside God. This chapter walks you through some elements of Jesus' divinity, including whether and why he was sent down from heaven to earth for purposes of salvation, whether he did miracles and whether he died for the sins of humanity. Since this book is not intended to cover these matters in full detail, only minimal summary explanations are given related to each question. The goal of this chapter is to help you face what you do and do not believe about the central figure of Christianity.

A **first** question about Jesus is when his existence began. Some early Christians believed and some didn't believe that Jesus existed with God before the creation of the world. They got into big fights over that statement, because some people said, "Jesus didn't exist with God before the creation of the world because God created Jesus." But those who believed that Jesus is co-eternal with God said, "No, no, no! You can't do that. If Jesus is divine, Jesus had to exist with God before the creation of the world."

Therefore, what we have in the very beginning of the Gospel of John is called the "gnostic hymn." It says, "In the beginning was the Word, and the Word was with God, and the Word was God" (John 1:1). That is to say, Jesus existed with God from the beginning, before the creation of the world, was not a part of creation, was not created by God. Those who believed that Jesus was divine said, "He can't be a creature." Anything that's created is a creature, and creatures aren't divine. And so the battle raged.

In fact, there were those in the early Christian church who said that God stood at the center of creation, and Jesus was God's right hand or *logos*." *Logos* means "word." It means more than that, actually. *Logos* also means "mind," "will," "brain" and/or "identity." It's really a comprehensive word in Greek. They used it in a variety of ways with a multitude of meanings.

A **second** point of debate is that Jesus was sent down by God from heaven to earth to be the savior of the world . Those who focus on the divine side are big on this understanding. These thought forms have a blended history.

Until 500 BCE, the major world religions were about the number ONE. The important number was one. Even in Hinduism, the big number was one, even though there are millions of gods in Hinduism. Those millions of gods can be seen as manifestations of one God. You had oneness in Buddhism, in Taoism, in Confucianism. Each human being is whole and not divided into two or three parts, like mind, body and soul. The universe is one and not divided into heaven and earth.

In ancient Hebrew thought and in the religion which became known as Judaism (which also began around 500 BCE), the number is one. There is one god. Deuteronomy 6:4 says, "Hear, O Israel. The Lord is our God. The Lord is one!" So, the early Jewish Christians believed in one God in Jerusalem. But not the Roman Christians. Rome had many gods with power over different areas of life. And there was no way that a human being, particularly a Jew from a backwater province like Galilee, was going to compete with those gods in Rome, unless that Palestinian Jew was also a very powerful god.

However, in Persian Zoroastrianism, which started around 550 BCE, there were two gods. Angra Mainyu was the bad god, and Ahura Mazda was the good god. They were almost equal, but Ahura Mazda had a little bit of an edge. They and their armies were in constant cosmic battle. Ahura Mazda created the Earth and its people as a trap for Angra Mainyu. This battle between the good god and the bad god provided the need for a savior figure for human beings.

So, Ahura Mazda sent one of his Six Holy Immortals, Mithras, down to Earth to teach human beings how to live moral, noble lives, and by doing so help defeat the god of immorality, Angra Mainyu. Mithraism became a sub-religion of Zoroastrianism, particularly in the Roman army. Mithraism became Christianity's chief competitor in the first 200 years of Christianity. Roman soldiers became infatuated with the idea of this divine/human figure, who led them in battle, symbolically speaking. (Eventually, Christians were able to convince them that Jesus was Mithras.)

The concept of a divine/human savior figure also arose in Gnosticism. In Gnosticism, the divine figure was sent down from the *pleroma*, where all the gods lived. He was sent down in human form to teach secret magic words to human beings who needed them when they died in order to get into heaven. In Gnostic thought, humans were created with an innate divine "spark," which was imprisoned in the body during one's life. Since the body (or "flesh") was regarded as a stinking prison for the divine "spark" or "soul," the soul longed to be free from the garbage heap of a body. The only way to be free was to learn the magic words taught by the divine/human figure, and the enlightened soul of a dead human could recite these passwords to get through the gates of the seven heavens and eventually allow a return to the *pleroma*, or ultimate heaven.

On the other hand, Hebrew prophetic literature endorsed the concept of a *messiah* to be raised up from among the common people as a savior of the people. This thoroughly human being would be chosen by God and anointed to accomplish a special purpose in God's will. In fact, the literature contains the stories of several *messiahs*, from Kings Saul and David to the Persian king, Cyrus the Great (Isaiah 45:1). Nowhere in the Old Testament is there a concept of a god being sent down from heaven to save the people, except in the disputed book of Daniel, which has Zoroastrian overtones. Rather, the human *messiah* exerts responsibility on God's behalf. In Hebrew thinking, this responsibility always involved issues of social justice and reform with spiritual and ethical repercussions.

At the time of Jesus, the Jewish people were hoping for the arrival of a new *messiah*, who would gather and command a huge army and drive the occupying Romans out of Palestine. Such a leader was to arrive in Jerusalem, riding on a donkey. This "king" would not be a "son of God" but would be a "son of Adam" or "son of man." He would free the people from social, religious and political oppression, and all people of the world would experience peace and justice.

The **third** point of contention is whether Jesus entered the world as a baby but with full divine knowledge and power. Since knowledge was the highest valued commodity of Jesus' time, this is not an insignificant question. Those who understand Jesus to be God's *logos* (mind) are certain that Jesus brought the wisdom of the spheres with him to the manger in Bethlehem. There was nothing Jesus did not know throughout his lifetime in human form.

This argument is countered by one little verse in Luke 2:52, which says that "Jesus grew in wisdom." Growing in wisdom meant that he wasn't born with full knowledge and wisdom, but that he picked up more as he went.

The **fourth** area of disagreement about Jesus is the concept of the "Virgin Birth." Those who believed in the divinity of Jesus held fervently to the idea that Jesus was conceived by the Holy Spirit of God and was born of Mary, who had never engaged in human sexual intercourse with Joseph or any other man. Those who were more impressed with the humanity of Jesus understood his birth story to be a fairly typical Middle Eastern "hero birth story," like the birth stories of Moses and Samson, with pieces added from the stories of the Greek gods on Mt. Olympus. This group also pointed out that the genealogies of Jesus in Matthew 1 and Luke 3 came through Joseph's side of the family, which makes Jesus a member of the tribe of Judah and the house of David. Both tribe and house were necessary to be the expected *messiah*. Tradition has Mary belonging to the tribe of Benjamin.

A common misconception is that the concept of the "immaculate conception" refers to the immaculate conception of Jesus. This Catholic doctrine refers to the conception of Mary by her parents, which was believed to have made her a fit vessel to be the mother of Jesus. The ideas behind this doctrine come from the "tradition" of the Catholic Church and not from the Bible.

A **fifth** problem with the divinity of Jesus is in the language proposed to say that Jesus is the "only-begotten" Son of God. While this phrase is not found in the best modern translations of the Bible, it is prominent in the Nicene Creed, written in 325 by a council of Christian bishops for use by congregations in worship services. The word "begotten" was a handy word in Greek, because it could mean either "born" or "adopted" or "claimed." These meanings satisfied both sides of the issue over the pre-existence of Jesus with God, the first problem in this chapter. But it was clear that they had to establish Jesus as not only a son of God, but he had to be the one and only Son of God. Without this claim, it would have been hard to claim that Jesus was the Savior of the world.

The fly in this ointment is that the Bible itself speaks of many other "sons of God." The words in Hebrew are *b'nai-elohim*. These words are used in a curious passage in the sixth chapter of Genesis, describing some men who appeared out of nowhere to marry the daughters of Adam and Eve. Another story at the beginning of the Book of Job tells of the "sons of God" having two meetings with God. A king is called a "son of God" in Psalm 2:7. Also, Adam is referred to as "son of God" in Luke 3:38.

The **sixth** question is whether Jesus performed many physical miracles, e.g. healing the sick, walking on water, raising people from the dead. The Gospel of Mark is especially full of miracles, indicating the gospel's interest in demonstrating that Jesus is the divine Son of God. There were many other gods in the Graeco-Roman world who could do marvelous and miraculous things. Jesus had to be able to compete with them and their power, at least in the minds of the believers.

The Greeks' most famous legendary healer was Asclepius, son of Apollo. Asclepius was the god of healing, and his best-known healing center was near Corinth, Greece. Jesus had to prove himself at least an equal to Asclepius. Poseidon was the Greek god of the seas. Neptune was his Roman counterpart. They controlled the seas, everything that happened in and on the oceans. Jesus, therefore, must be able to calm the winds and the waves on the Sea of Galilee. His walking on the water is further proof that he is in the same league with Poseidon and Neptune.

Apollonius was a contemporary of Jesus. He was an itinerant teacher around Rome. He was thought to be the incarnation of an Egyptian god, Proteus. He is reported by Philostratus to have raised people from the dead, notably a young bride who died on her wedding day. This legend would have been circulated throughout the Roman Empire, making essential the inclusion of stories of Jesus' miracles of resurrection.

The **seventh** area of concern about the divinity of Jesus is centered around the Doctrine of Atonement, which ends with the statement that Jesus was crucified as the lamb without blemish to take away the sins of the world. This claims that the agonizing death of Jesus, who was the only one to live a life without sin, was necessary as the sacrifice to atone for sins of all humankind against God for all time. There are several variations of the Doctrine of Atonement, and this one is called "substitutionary atonement."

While the Doctrine of Atonement is a bedrock doctrine of Christianity, many questions have been raised about it through the centuries, particularly questions about the nature of God that it assumes. It is God who is said to be the one who needs to be satisfied, who demands a blood sacrifice because the people have sinned. So this God sends his only son to die a horrible death on the cross to satisfy the needs of this God. The cosmic Department of Justice, presided over by this God, requires that humanity be destroyed as punishment for crimes committed against God, but God promised after the great flood of Noah never again to destroy the human race. So, since God loves humankind so much, God sent God's only son down from heaven as the sacrificial lamb to be killed to appease God's own anger toward humans, because they have wronged God grievously.

The problem for some is that they cannot buy into this doctrine for several reasons. One reason is that atonement begins with the concept of the "fall of humanity" in the Garden of Eden, the "original sin" of eating the apple in direct disobedience of God, who told them not to eat from the apple tree. Sometimes ignored in this story is the fact that Adam and Eve didn't know the difference between good and bad until **after** they had eaten the fruit from the Tree of the Knowledge of Good and Bad. Therefore, they couldn't have willfully disobeyed. They were newborns. Would a loving God punish a fifteen-minute-old baby for disobedience? Would you?

The entire issue of the death of Jesus raised many questions in the early Christian movement. How could a god die? Gods are, by definition, immortal, meaning "not mortal." A significant group of early Christians, led by a teacher named Marcion, believed that Jesus remained a god the entire time he was on earth and simply appeared to be a human. Therefore, he only appeared to die on the cross. Marcion's group was the Docetics, from the Latin word *doceo*, which means "to seem or appear." They were declared heretics by the establishment. In an early creed written to be recited by individuals being baptized, the "Apostles' Creed," it is stated in four ways that Jesus really died, primarily to contradict the Docetics. The creed says that Jesus was "crucified, dead and buried. He descended into Hell (understood to be the place where all dead people went)." Early Christians who opposed the Docetics wanted new candidates for baptism to have the correct understanding of Jesus' death.

The **eighth** point emphasized by those who stress the divinity of Jesus is that he was raised miraculously and wonderfully from the tomb in a physical body, and he appeared to and talked with his female followers and his male disciples. The physical resurrection of Jesus is the *sine qua non* (essential belief) of Christianity. A dead god is no god at all. A resurrected god is special, having conquered Death.

Belief in Jesus' physical resurrection is difficult, if not impossible, for many, because it does not relate to the clay of people's experience. The apostle Paul felt a need to argue vociferously for the physical resurrection, recognizing that it would take a lot of repetition to sell what he believed to be the truth.

The matter of the nature of the resurrected body got a split decision. The Gospel of Luke says that Jesus walks through walls and doors and appears and disappears at will, indicating a spiritual body, but Luke and the Gospel of John also say that Jesus ate fish with a very physical body.

The **ninth** and last problem (that we will deal with in this book) with Jesus as divine Son of God is the contention that Jesus went back up into heaven and sits at the right hand of God the Father. As pointed out in the chapter on the Bible, the gospels of Luke and Matthew disagree on where Jesus was when he went back up into heaven. Luke says he "ascended" from Bethany, just outside Jerusalem, in Judea. Matthew says he spoke his farewells on an unnamed mountain in Galilee, perhaps Mt. Tabor, 100 kilometers (60 miles) north of Jerusalem as the crow flies.

The image of Jesus sitting at the right hand of God evokes the scene of a throne room. The monarch (God) sits on the big throne in the middle, up on the royal dais, and the crown prince (Jesus) sits in the throne of the designated successor, on the king's right. The occupant of the throne on the left is not mentioned, but speculation would place Holy Spirit or Wisdom in that chair.

One could list several other problems that have been encountered through the centuries concerning Jesus as divine Son of God, but nine will suffice. However, there is one more story that is worth knowing that illustrates the context in which the story of Jesus was written.

> **The story of Dionysus is a legend that was popular in the Graeco-Roman world in the time of Jesus. According to the legend, Dionysus was part god and part human, the son of Zeus, the chief god on Mt. Olympus, who impregnated the virgin daughter of the King of Thebes. When Dionysus was born, Zeus' wife, Hera, learned that her husband had been unfaithful to her and sent her minions to kill the baby. They were unsuccessful. Dionysus grew up to be a renowned teacher of agriculture, especially wine-making, but at a relatively young age was tortured and killed. At his death, Zeus revived him and brought him to Mt. Olympus, placing him in the seat of honor at Zeus' right hand. The Romans adopted Dionysus as a hero god, whose symbol was a goat, since the story portrays him as an innocent scapegoat who was sacrificed on behalf of others.**

It is important to understand that one may embrace all these notions about the divinity of Jesus, as probably the majority of Christians do. The purpose of this chapter is to let you know some background information behind these concepts, and to point out where some problems are. This way, you can make an informed choice about what you believe.

Likewise, one may reject one or all of these concepts. One may not believe Jesus to be the only divine Son of God. Most people whom I have met who choose not to be involved in the institutional church do not believe in the divinity of Jesus. Generally speaking, these same people have great admiration for the human Jesus and his teachings. This is the most definitive issue dividing churched and unchurched people in the United States today.

The material in this chapter is straw. Does any of it touch your clay?

8. IS THERE A PROBLEM WITH JESUS AS "THE DIVINE SON OF GOD?"

Concerning the divinity of Jesus:
I believe (or not) that Jesus existed with God before the creation of the world. Why?

I believe (or not) that Jesus was sent down by God from heaven to be the savior of the world. Why?

I believe (or not) that Jesus entered the world as a baby but with full divine knowledge and power. Why?

I believe (or not) that Jesus was conceived by the Holy Spirit, and born of Mary who had never engaged in human sexual intercourse. Why?

I believe (or not) that Jesus is the only-begotten Son of God. Why?

I believe (or not) that Jesus performed many physical miracles, e.g. healing, walking on water, raising Lazarus from the dead. Why?

I believe (or not) that sinless Jesus was crucified as the lamb without blemish to take away the sins of the world. Why?

I believe (or not) that Jesus was resurrected by God from the tomb with the same physical body he had earlier. Why?

I believe (or not) that Jesus went back up into heaven and sits at the right hand of God the Father. Why?

CHAPTER 9
IS IT ENOUGH FOR JESUS TO BE A HUMAN MESSIAH?

> A young man told me recently that his idea of Jesus was like one of those big balloon figures in Macy's Thanksgiving Day Parade. He said that Jesus wasn't just bigger than life but hugely inflated. However, he went on to say that his Jesus balloon had now sprung a leak and deflated to the ground, because he could no longer believe in Jesus as a god. "I have to find a new Jesus," he said.

Marcus Borg's book, *Finding Jesus Again for the First Time* (HarperCollins, 1994) has helped many people find Jesus again for the first time. The Jesus Seminar, made up of around 80 international New Testament scholars, is raising new issues and old eyebrows about what the historical Jesus may have really said and done. Professor Borg, who teaches at Oregon State University, is one of the most famous of these scholars.

The thesis of Borg's book is that Christians must do more than believe things about Jesus. He talks about "giving one's heart" to Jesus in the sense of experiencing Jesus in his life relationship with God. He calls this "moving from secondhand religion to firsthand religion," which I call "building personal faith with a passion." Bob Funk says in *Honest to Jesus* (HarperCollins, 1996) that Christians need to stand beside Jesus and point with him, our index fingers alongside his, toward God and the Kingdom of Heaven instead of pointing at Jesus' finger. Christianity has become very Christocentric, or Jesus-centered, instead of God-centered. This occurred because Christians have pointed at Jesus' finger rather than standing beside Jesus and pointing toward God.

Jesus was pointing toward God spiritually just as you use your index finger to point toward something you want another person to experience. You want that person to experience the object at which you are pointing. You don't want that person to stare at your index finger.

The humanity of Jesus is much more palatable to non-Christians and Christians who choose not to be involved in churches. The human Jesus is affirmed and appreciated by most of Judaism and Islam. The mixing of humanity with divinity is the controversial issue, begging for paradoxical status, while the rest of the world observes a contradiction with monotheism. Many non-Christians see Christianity as a religion with two or three or more gods.

Most of the creeds of the Christian church speak of Jesus' two natures, divine and human, and say that they were both "perfect" and "complete." The statement is made and the Church teaches that Jesus was "wholly God and wholly human."

They didn't agree on the nature of Jesus in the early Christian church. That was the initial conflict over the issue of the humanity or divinity of Jesus. There was James, who was the leader of the church in Jerusalem. James was Jesus' brother. He saw Jesus as human, as did Peter, in whose home in Capernaum Jesus may have lived his adult life.

On the other hand, there was Paul, who never met Jesus in the flesh. Paul never saw the human Jesus. Paul's experience of Jesus was of a god, the risen Christ, when he experienced the return of Jesus to him on the Damascus road. He understood Jesus to be divine. The human Jesus is not very important to Paul. The divine Jesus is everything to Paul. But, to the church in Jerusalem, the human Jesus is important. And that conflict in experience continued throughout early Christianity, the battle between Christians in Jerusalem and Christians in other places, like Rome and Ephesus.

As we examine a few events in the story of Jesus, see if there are points where you can identify with a human Jesus. After all, it's necessary to identify with someone before you can be committed to that person. You love the one you know, who is the one with whom you identify, who is the one with whom you have shared experiences.

Jesus' Baptism

The baptism of Jesus can be a shared experience, in a symbolic sense. According to the biblical story, John the Baptizer baptized Jesus in the River Jordan near Jericho after Jesus had attended the Temple in Jerusalem, doing his duty at the Passover. There are symbols everywhere in this story. The Jordan River stands for an entrance into a new place and symbolizes the Sea of Reeds at the time of the Exodus. John is the symbol of Moses, who parted the "Sea of Reeds," and Elijah, who was also a denizen of the Jordan, and who, according to Hebrew scripture, must precede the Messiah.

Three very eloquent symbols present themselves at the time of Jesus' baptism. First, the dome of the sky was ripped open by God, in apparent impatience to touch Jesus. Secondly, the Spirit of God descended through this hole in the sky in the form of a dove and landed on Jesus. The climax and meaning of the whole event is the third symbol, and that is the claiming and affirmation of Jesus by God with the words, "This is my child, whom I love unconditionally." (This is one of only three lines God speaks in all the gospels.)

If you have been baptized, if you were dedicated, if you have experienced God's claiming of you and the expression of God's unconditional love for you, then you can identify with Jesus in his baptism. Does this straw touch your clay?

Some scholars say that Jesus' baptism is the moment when Jesus was anointed Messiah. Certainly, the gospels say that Jesus (quit his job as a stone mason in Capernaum, I believe, and) began his ministry shortly after his baptism. But first, there was temptation in the wilderness.

Jesus' Temptation

The wilderness of Judea is west of Jericho and east of Jerusalem, and the well-traveled "Jericho road" (actually a path) up or down 4,000 feet, connecting the two cities, runs through it. King Herod built an aqueduct through this wilderness, on the side of a wadi, to provide water for his winter palace in Jericho. In most places, this wilderness is so barren it looks like moonscape, with only rocks and sand showing. There are many caves in the limestone rock.

Here, Jesus experienced temptation, symbolized by the tempter, the devil, or Satan, three different names given by Mark, Matthew, and Luke. After a long time without food (40 days and 40 nights is a Hebrew idiom meaning "a long time"), he was tempted to abandon his fasting and prove his power by turning rocks into bread. It is obvious that the real temptation was to put material things in a higher priority than spiritual matters, because Jesus answered by saying that a person doesn't live primarily by bread. What is primary in one's life is the word of God, or inspiration or revelation or spirituality.

For his second temptation, Jesus was mysteriously transported to Jerusalem and placed on top of the wall on the southeast corner of the Temple Mount, overlooking the Kidron Valley. He was tempted to jump off and trust God to keep him from being injured in a sure-fire suicide leap. The temptation was to be irresponsible for himself and thereby to test the power of God to pull his fat out of the fire. Jesus answered by quoting a famous line from the Torah, "You don't test God."

His last temptation occurred on a very high mountain, perhaps Mt. Hermon in Syria, to which he was again transported mysteriously. Looking down on the rest of the world, he was tempted to become temporal ruler of the Earth by taking governmental responsibility for all people. He answered by saying that he worshiped and served God alone, not temptation and not himself. He neither wanted nor needed to take political responsibility for people God had not made him responsible for, because to do so would be to play God.

If you are ever tempted to put material things in front of your spiritual life, you can identify with the first temptation of Jesus. If you are ever tempted to be irresponsible for your actions and decisions and test God to get you out of it, you can identify with the second temptation. If you are ever tempted to take on responsibility **for** someone God hasn't made you responsible for, like a healthy spouse or a mature child, then you have tried to play God, and you can identify with number three. These are three killer temptations. If you succumb to any one of them during the course of a day, you can lose the day.

It is very interesting where Jesus got the verses of scripture he quoted in answering the temptations. All three come from Deuteronomy, chapters 6 and 8, and all are part of the Great Shema, which was and is the first thing memorized by Hebrew children. Jesus didn't have to go past his childhood ABC's to find the straw he had mixed with his clay to form the belief bricks he needed at that important moment to defeat deadly temptations.

Jesus' Spiritual Death

Jesus was crucified outside the city wall of Jerusalem. There are differences of opinion as to who was responsible for his death: Jews, Romans or God. (I opt for the Romans.) There are various ideas as to where and how the Romans crucified Jews at Jerusalem. The traditional view is the "old rugged cross" on top of a hill called "Calvary." A more recent understanding has emerged that the Romans employed the scaffolding down at the base of a rock quarry to hoist up a condemned man, attached by nails or rope to a single piece of wood. The theory is that the Romans chose the rock quarry because this was the same place the Jews brought their condemned to stone them to death, thereby making it a "killing field." It was called "Golgotha," which means "the place of the skull" because of all the skulls lying around.

When a man was crucified, he endured great agony until his lungs collapsed and he could no longer breathe. He was lucky if the Romans broke his legs since that hastened his death. If he found any kind of foothold, he could push his body up, relieve his lungs and the agony could last for days. Meanwhile, since every crucified man was naked and defenseless, large birds could have what they wanted from him. The biblical story says that Jesus was crucified at 9:00 in the morning and breathed his last breath at 3:00 in the afternoon, a merciful six hours, especially since his legs were reportedly not broken.

The picture of Jesus' death has become one of the most poignant pictures of the religious world. The symbol of the cross has become one of the most, if not **the** most, recognizable symbols in all the world. There are different meanings for different people: death, salvation, forgiveness, sacrifice, the worst of life. The problem is we cannot experience physical death with Jesus and still have this conversation. We have to examine what was going on in Jesus' spiritual world, his spiritual death, while he was dying physically.

> **It was already about noon, and darkness blanketed the whole land until mid-afternoon, during an eclipse of the sun. And at three o'clock in the afternoon Jesus shouted at the top of his voice (the 22nd Psalm, entitled)** *"Eli, Eli, lema sabachthani?"*, **which says (in the most significant verses),**
>
> **"My God, my God, why did you abandon me?**
> **Why aren't you helping me?**
> **Why aren't you listening to my groans?**
> **My God, I pray all day long, but you don't answer!**
> **I pray all night long, and can't go to sleep!**
> **I'm a worm and not a human being.**
> **People shun me and they despise me.**
> **Everybody who sees me makes fun of me.**
> **They stick out their tongues at me.**
> **They make vile gestures at me.**
> **They tell me to trust in the Lord,**
> **That he will rescue me if he likes me.**
> **All the terrible things happening to me**
> **Are like mad bulls charging me,**

Or like a roaring and hungry lion about to eat me.
Physically, I'm as weak as water.
All my bones feel like they are out of joint.
My heart is like melted wax in my chest.
My mouth is as dry as dust,
And my tongue sticks to the inside of my mouth.
You have let me die!
Sons-of-bitches are all around me!
My hands and feet have shriveled.
I look like a skeleton.
People stare at me and they're thrilled
that I look this way.
(My translation/paraphrase)

The words of the Psalm indicate that Jesus was experiencing despair and hopelessness. In a spiritual sense, he experienced the absence of God in his world.

Can you identify with this experience? Has there been a time in your life when you were willing to give up, pack it in, lie down and quit? In Alcoholics Anonymous, this is called "hitting the wall." In other literature, it's called "the dark night of the soul." It happens very often in concert with one's initial profound encounter with one's mortality, when you really, really realize that one day you will die physically, and you ask the question of the meaning of life and cannot find the answer. Does this straw touch your clay? (There is much more about this in Chapter 17.)

Jesus' Spiritual Resurrection

A great preacher proclaimed, "It's Friday, but Sunday's a-coming." Friday, known as "Good Friday" in Christendom, symbolizes spiritual death, the worst of life. Sunday, the first day of the week, is known as "the Lord's Day" because of the assertion in the Gospels that Jesus rose physically from the tomb before dawn on Easter Sunday. Sunday was then chosen as the day of Christian worship rather than the Sabbath of the Jews. Sunday symbolizes new life, the best of life, and the Church calls Christians to celebrate Easter each Sunday, the day formally set aside to celebrate resurrected living, which Easter symbolizes.

There is no record of what Jesus thought and felt about having been resurrected. But there are a few recorded comments about how Jesus' male disciples and female followers felt when they learned of Jesus' resurrection. In a very significant way, the disciples and the women had experienced spiritual death with Jesus since they believed they had lost their teacher, on whom they had bet the farm. Their entire reason for being was dead. To describe Jesus' closest followers on the first Easter, the gospel writers used words like "joyful" and "amazed" and "wondering" but also "startled" and "disbelieving" and "terrified." From Jesus' disciples and followers and from the story of the life of Jesus prior to his death and resurrection, we can begin to understand what it feels like to be spiritually resurrected.

Mary Magdalene had suddenly felt a great void, but now that void was filled with love. Simon Peter had suddenly felt the crush of guilt, fear and defeat, but now sensed the hope of victory. Mary, the mother of Jesus, had experienced the cruel death of her first-born son and had entered the spinning vortex of meaningless, but now found new meaning in her life. These three, along with the other disciples and women, were changed forever, willing and ready to proclaim and die for what they had experienced.

The story of the life of Jesus shows how to live as a spiritually resurrected person. It is life in the presence of God in the Kingdom of Heaven. It is life that is dominated by faith. It is life that has meaning and purpose. It is loving and caring, healing and teaching. It is believing that God has made available all the great intangible gifts. It is accepting these gifts with thanksgiving. That's spiritual life.

Does this straw touch your clay? Jean-Paul Sartre said that "life begins on the far side of despair." He was writing about spiritual resurrection. Almost all the great classics of literature and film are on this theme, and many of the musical classics are also. It's about life after death in this life. (There is much more about this in Chapter 18.)

Jesus' Transfiguration

Six days (into this journey), Jesus took with him Peter and James and John, and led them off by themselves, (climbing) to (the top of) a lofty mountain to pray. While he was praying, he was transformed in front of them, and his face took on a strange appearance and it shone like the sun. His clothing turned dazzling white, whiter than any laundry on earth could make them.

The next thing you know, two figures appeared in glory, Moses and Elijah, and they were talking to Jesus. They were discussing his departure, which he was destined to carry out in Jerusalem.

Peter and those who were with him were half asleep at the time, but they came wide awake when they saw his glory and the two men standing next to him. As the men were leaving him, Peter said to Jesus, "Master, it's a good thing we are here. In fact, why not set up three tents, one for you, one for Moses and one for Elijah!" He didn't know what he was saying, because they were scared to death.

While he was still speaking, a bright cloud moved in and cast a shadow over them. And their fear increased as they entered the cloud. A voice spoke out of the cloud, and said, "This is my Son, my Beloved, of whom I fully approve. Listen to him!"

> When the disciples heard the voice speaking, they prostrated themselves. But Jesus came and touched them, and said, "Get up! Don't be afraid." And when they looked up, they saw no one except Jesus by himself.

This is the merged account of the transfiguration of Jesus from Matthew 17:1-8, Mark 9:2-8 and Luke 9:28-36.

It is a "mountain-top experience." Jesus is witnessed to be in the presence of Moses, who represents the Torah, or Teaching, or Law; and Elijah, who represents the Prophets, or books of prophecy and history. These books together made up Jesus' Bible, his scripture, the Law and the Prophets.

Moses and Elijah also represent souls that wander freely through the universe. According to the biblical account in II Kings 2, Elijah was taken away from Elisha, his protegé, in a fiery chariot. He was not observed to die and was not buried. Moses went up on Mt. Nebo to look over at the Promised Land, which he was forbidden to enter, and was said to have died there, but his burial place was unknown. Therefore, these two loose spirits show up with Jesus in a high and holy moment.

How can you follow that? How can you identify with that experience?

Have you ever had an experience when you felt the presence of God, the closer than which you cannot imagine? That's transfiguration. You don't cause a moment like that to happen. It just happens, and you and God are as one. It is a mystical moment when ordinary time stands still, when the hair rises on the back of your neck. It is a rare event of perfect peace and tranquility, pure love and heightened consciousness.

Notice that God speaks virtually the same line in the transfiguration story as God speaks in the baptism story: "This is my child, whom I love unconditionally." Here again is the ultimate claiming by God which you and Jesus can share experientially. Does this straw touch your clay?

You commit yourself to a person you love. You love a person you know. You know a person with whom you have shared important experiences. That's where the identification comes from. It's impossible to sing "O, How I Love Jesus" with maturity and integrity unless and until you have had important shared experiences with Jesus.

Is it enough for Jesus to be human messiah? Is it enough for Jesus to be God's universal symbol of the reality of spiritual death and the hope of spiritual resurrection, the crucial events in the life of every human being on the planet? Is it enough for Jesus to symbolize something greater than he was? Is it enough for Jesus to show you how to pass through the portal to life as God wishes everyone to live?

9. IS IT ENOUGH FOR JESUS TO BE A HUMAN MESSIAH?

Concerning the humanity of Jesus:
I believe (or not) that Jesus was a Jew raised up by God to be the savior of the world. Why?

I believe (or not) that Jesus experienced every human emotion possible. Why?

I believe (or not) that Jesus grew up as a human and learned as he went. Why?

I believe (or not) that Jesus was claimed by God at the time of his baptism. Why?

I believe (or not) that Jesus was tempted to do the wrong things all humans are tempted to do, and he refused to do them. Why?

I believe (or not) that Jesus accepted the great intangible gifts of God in an unprecedented manner and quantity. Why?

I believe (or not) that Jesus died physically on the cross. Why?

I believe (or not) that Jesus experienced spiritual death as well as physical death on the cross. Why?

I believe (or not) that Jesus experienced spiritual resurrection after his spiritual death. Why?

CHAPTER 10
WHERE IN THE WORLD DID HOLY SPIRIT COME FROM?

There has been much controversy about the nature, work, and personhood of Holy Spirit since the beginning of Christianity. Here are six of the most critical issues.

First, there is a need for definition. Holy Spirit can be translated from Hebrew or Greek as "sacred breath of life." The word "spirit" in Hebrew is either *ruach* or *nephesh*, in Greek *pneuma*. All three words mean "moving air," either wind or breath. These three words are directly related to life itself.

How did people back in biblical days know if you were alive or dead? Did they check your pulse? Did they give you an EKG or an EEG? No, if you were breathing, you were alive. Where did that breath come from? It came from God and it was God's breath of life. If you accept that premise, then everything that lives and breathes is filled with Holy Spirit, the sacred breath of all breathing organisms.

While I was writing this, I got a call from a good friend whose husband was in the emergency room at the hospital. His heart had stopped as he was in the shower. My friend heard him fall in the bathroom, rushed to his side and did everything she could do to revive him. The paramedics did their best and transported him to the hospital, but he had no brain function when they examined him. They got his heart beating again and put him on a ventilator. I hurried to the hospital and got there just as he breathed out his last breath on his own before the ventilator had to take over breathing him. The sacred breath of life left him. He was no longer alive. He had a living will, stating that he was not to be breathed artificially. They pulled the plug and a short time later, all body functions stopped. God didn't leave him, just the sacred breath of life.

What's *pneuma*? The basic sense of this Greek word is the function of a pneumatic drill, a tool that's air-driven, using moving air. This concept of moving air is helpful in understanding the Stoic belief in *pneuma*. In biblical times, the Stoics in Rome believed that the whole cosmos was made up of two kinds of matter: passive matter and active matter. The active matter they called *pneuma*, the fiery spirit or breath which creates and gives form to matter and causes it to stick together. The Stoics taught that this spirit functions in the universe just like the soul does in human body, providing life and harmony.

The early Christian church in Rome was heavily influenced by Stoic thinking. Because of this, the concept of the Spirit of God became an important concept in the Roman church, and the Roman church became more and more influential in Christian theology as time went along. It could be that the Roman church lobbied hard for the inclusion of Holy Spirit as one of the three primary manifestations of God, along with Father and Son.

Secondly, there is the question of the work of Holy Spirit. Some consider Holy Spirit as the gift of revelation from God. When God says or reveals anything to you, it is the work of Holy Spirit. When you read anything important to you in the Bible, or hear anything important to you in a sermon or discussion or lecture, it's the work of Holy Spirit. You might say that whenever someone's straw touches your clay with an important message, which supplies you with what is clearly truth to you, that is revelation and the work of Holy Spirit. When the answer comes to a very important life question, that may be the work of Holy Spirit. When you find clarity on some issue of concern where before there was only murky water, that may be the work of Holy Spirit. This is why many theologians refer to Holy Spirit as "the Revealer."

Thirdly, the second chapter of Acts tells the story of Holy Spirit coming like a tornado, together with lightning, and touching Jesus' disciples. They were hunkered down in Jerusalem for fifty days after the resurrection of Jesus, waiting for "power from on high." This happened on the Day of Pentecost, an important Jewish festival, when all Jewish males were expected to be in Jerusalem. The story says that "all of them were filled with Holy Spirit and began to speak in other (known) languages, as the Spirit gave them ability," i.e. Holy Spirit gave the disciples supernatural abilities. This is also about the work of Holy Spirit.

The miraculous thing about this story is that Jesus' disciples began to speak in all kinds of different languages they had never heard or spoken before. These are not educated men, even though the most uneducated people of first century Palestine spoke three or four languages fluently, including Aramaic at home, Greek in the marketplace, Latin to the authorities, and Hebrew in the Temple. But for them to speak boldly in many other languages is a miracle. The story goes on to tell of their courage in the face of persecution, even to their martyrdom.

There are two tornados mentioned in the Bible. The Pentecost tornado is one. The other one is in one of the creation stories in Genesis. The older creation story in most versions of the Bible says that God came calling in the Garden of Eden at the time of the "evening breeze," but the Hebrew says that the "evening breeze" was "a mighty wind" (Genesis 3:8). The implication is that it was actually a tornado. Both were frightening events.

Fourthly, not only do some Christians believe that Holy Spirit gives the power to speak in unknown languages, but also to heal physically sick or wounded people by the laying on of hands, to exorcize demons by prayer and anointing and laying on of hands, to be bitten by poisonous snakes or drink poison with impunity. That's what it says in the longer ending of Mark (16:9-20), which is not included in the best ancient manuscripts.

> **An old 45 rpm record tells the story of the guy who went to one of those "Holy Ghost" churches in east Tennessee, where they were handling snakes. The friend who invited him to church that Sunday night didn't tell him they were going to do that. He was sitting there in the pew, close to the front of the church, when suddenly here came a man carrying**

a box of snakes. People began coming to the front and reaching in and taking out five-foot-long timber rattlesnakes and holding them up with their tails a-rattling.

He said to his friend, "Where do you want a new door in this church building? I'm gonna make you one."

Fifthly, in John 14:26, Jesus is quoted as saying that "the Holy Spirit, whom the Father will send, identical to me (in my name), will teach you everything, and remind you of all that I have said to you." But one chapter later, in John 15:26, Jesus is quoted as saying, "When the Helper comes, whom I will send to you from the Father, the Spirit of Truth who comes from the Father, he will testify on my behalf." What does that mean to you, and do you see a little contradiction between those two statements?

Lastly, Holy Spirit is referred to as the "Third Person of the Trinity." John Dominic Crossan, Professor Emeritus at DePaul University, says that, for most Christians, Holy Spirit is just a polite way of saying "I don't know." One of the problems Christians have had with Holy Spirit through the ages is that they've never been given a picture of Holy Spirit, and most people have pictures of their god or gods, Judaism and Islam being notable exceptions. Gods are pictured throughout the history of the civilizations of Egypt and Mesopotamia. Greek and Roman gods appeared in carvings, paintings and statues. If people today don't have an image of a god, that god probably doesn't exist in their minds.

There is a picture of God on the ceiling of the Sistine Chapel in Rome. Michelangelo painted it. It was very controversial when it was first unveiled because of the Old Testament prohibition against an image of God. Michelangelo painted God reaching out to Adam. Who does it look like? It's Charlton Heston, as Moses. So, we have that picture of God as the "Ancient of Days," with long white hair, moustache and beard, and white robe.

There are many pictures of Jesus. What's the most famous image of Jesus? Is it the crucifix? Is it da Vinci's *Last Supper*? Is it the other pictures of Jesus with all the European features, the Gentile look? But, where can you find a picture of the Holy Ghost? You can't and that's the problem. If somebody could paint a picture of Holy Spirit, many people would be more comfortable with the idea of Holy Spirit. But until that time, there's a big problem.

When I was a little kid, my picture of the Holy Ghost was Casper the Ghost, the cartoon character. You have to have pictures, and you don't have a picture of the Holy Ghost, unless you consider the dove to be that symbolic image. The dove can represent the quiet and pure presence of Holy Spirit or the dynamic, always moving activity of God.

Does any of this straw about Holy Spirit touch your clay? Have you experienced Holy Spirit? If so, how have you experienced it?

10. WHERE IN THE WORLD DID HOLY SPIRIT COME FROM?

"Holy Spirit" can be translated from Hebrew or Greek as "sacred breath of life." The word "spirit" in Hebrew is either *ruach* or *nephesh*, in Greek *pneuma*. All three words mean "moving air," either wind or breath. What does this mean to you?

Some consider Holy Spirit as the gift of revelation from God. When God says or reveals anything to you, it is the work of Holy Spirit. When you read anything important to you in the Bible, or hear anything important to you in a sermon, it is the work of Holy Spirit. Why do you agree or disagree with this?

The second chapter of Acts tells the story of Holy Spirit coming like a tornado, together with lightning, and touching Jesus' disciples. It says that "all of them were filled with Holy Spirit and began to speak in other languages, as the Spirit gave them ability," i.e. Holy Spirit gave the disciples supernatural abilities. Does Holy Spirit do that?

Pentecostals believe that Holy Spirit gives the power to speak in unknown languages, to heal physically sick or wounded people by the laying on of hands, to exorcise demons by prayer and anointing and laying on of hands, to be bitten by poisonous snakes or drink poison with impunity. Why do you agree or disagree with this?

In John 14:26, Jesus is quoted as saying that "the Holy Spirit, whom the Father will send, identical to me, will teach you everything, and remind you of all that I have said to you." In John 15:26, Jesus is quoted as saying, "When the Helper comes, whom I will send to you from the Father, the Spirit of Truth who comes from the Father, he will testify on my behalf." What does this mean to you?

Holy Spirit is referred to as the "Third Person of the Trinity." What does that mean to you? John Dominic Crossan says that, for most Christians, Holy Spirit is just a polite way of saying "I don't know." Do you agree or disagree with him?

CHAPTER 11
IS IT NECESSARY TO BELIEVE IN THE TRINITY?

The celebrated St. Augustine, Bishop of Hippo, said that Christians used the concept of Trinity and the word "Trinity" because "it was a little better than saying nothing, when one had to say something." (Source unknown) Nevertheless, he may have had more to do with the classic formulation of the Doctrine of the Trinity in the Latin language than anyone. Augustine presented the Roman Church with the idea of the Unknowable, Incomprehensible God, manifested equally and simultaneously as Father, Son, and Holy Spirit.

He said that God (*Deus*) is made known to humankind as the Father (*Pater*), that God is made known as Son (*Filius*), and that God is made known as Holy Spirit (*Spiritus Sanctus*). He also said that the Father is not the same as the Son and is not the same as the Holy Spirit. The Son is not the same as the Father or the Holy Spirit. The Holy Spirit is not the same as the Son or the Father. Around the year 400, the Roman Church adopted this doctrine. From the beginning of the fifth century to today, this has been and is the official Doctrine of the Trinity of Christianity.

Most Christians with whom I have discussed this teaching don't know how to state this doctrine or understand its subtleties. They have been taught that this is a paradox and a mystery which is to be accepted on blind faith. They recite the creeds and sing of "God in three persons, blessed Trinity," but don't really know what that means. It's hard to make a brick using straw that is religious information that doesn't make sense to you.

The majority of Christians today may be neither monotheistic nor trinitarian. Monotheism, the belief in the existence of one and only one God, may have been defeated by the emphasis in a large part of Christian teaching on Father, Son, and Holy Spirit as three distinct gods. The idea of the Trinity may have been defeated by a complete equation of God with the Father, to the exclusion of Jesus and the Holy Spirit.

Some Christians believe that the Trinity is a sequential matter, that God was made known to humankind as the Father before the time of Jesus (in Old Testament times), that God was made known as Jesus during the time of Jesus, and that God has been made known as the Holy Spirit since the time of Jesus. The "sequential Trinity" is different from the official version of this teaching.

In the original doctrine of the Trinity, there are four entities: Three in One, One in Three. God is the One in the classic trinitarian formula. God is "eternal, infinite, immeasurable, incomprehensible, omnipotent, invisible." These are adjectives describing God in a confession written when the Church of Scotland was being created in 1560. If you want to, you can think about this being the "Behind-the-Scenes" God.

But then, God is manifested. "Manifested" means "made visible," "made known," "shown forth," "demonstrated," "symbolized." God is manifested as the Father, as the Son, and as the Holy Spirit, equally and simultaneously manifested as three persons.

If you're a trinitarian, that's what you believe. If you do, you're unusual, because most Christians have put God and the Father totally together. What happens when you combine God and Father is that Jesus becomes a "stand-alone" god, rather than one of the three equal manifestations of God. In doing this, you have destroyed monotheism, because you don't have one God, manifested in three equal ways. You have one god here (God), one god there (the Father), and another god hanging out over yonder (Jesus). And Holy Spirit is "I don't know," because you don't have a picture. You've destroyed monotheism, and you've also destroyed the Trinity. [The third god of most American Christians is the Devil, a bad god. Most of American Christianity has two good gods (God and Jesus), one bad god (Devil), and then there is "I don't know."]

A hymn says, "God in Three Persons, Blessed Trinity." From your perspective, is there more emphasis on the one God or on the three Persons? Or, is the emphasis about equal? Some Muslims and some Jews will tell Christians to their faces, if asked, "Christianity has lost monotheism."

The biblical references to the three persons of the godhead are in a long discourse by Jesus in John 14-16; in a baptismal formula in Matthew 28:19, "baptizing them in the name of the Father, the Son, and the Holy Spirit"; and in a benediction in II Corinthians 13:13, the so-called "apostolic benediction": "The grace of the Lord Jesus Christ, the love of God, and the fellowship of the Holy Spirit be with you all." The word "trinity" does not occur in the New Testament.

The last two passages are said by many to be the two places where there is biblical substantiation of the trinitarian formula. However, these are triads. The difference between a triad and a trinity is that a triad is a cluster or group of three units. "Tri-unity" is what "trinity" comes from. The oneness is emphasized in a trinity. So, these passages speak of triads since the One factor is missing. The verse in Matthew would be trinitarian if it said, "Baptizing them in the name of God, manifested as Father, Son and Holy Spirit."

If Paul had said at the end of II Corinthians, "The grace of God, manifested in our Lord Jesus Christ, and the love of God, manifested in the Father, and the communion of God, manifested in Holy Spirit, be with you all," then it would be a trinitarian formula. But in their present form, they're triadic. Also, Paul has equated God with the Father, but remember that in Paul's time, the Doctrine of the Trinity had yet to be written.

Therefore, my point is that the Doctrine of the Trinity is not a biblically-based doctrine. The concept of Trinity seems to have arisen from conflict between the Hebrew thought world and the Greek thought world. The result may have been a compromise, political doctrine rather than a purely theological doctrine. Some scholars believe that the Doctrine of the Trinity was written in an attempt to reconcile Jewish Christians, with their strict belief in one God, with Gentile Christians, who needed Jesus to be the Son of God, a separate deity of their contemporary time. So again, we're talking about the Jewish Christians, the Gentile Christians, the fight within the early Christian church over this issue, the nature of Jesus and the nature of God.

That was a big fight in the early Christian church. And it is still a major controversy in contemporary Christian thought. The basic idea of the Doctrine of Trinity is that God reveals God equally as the Creator, Redeemer, Revealer; or Father, Son, Holy Spirit. In other words, with equal emphasis, God is manifested as Creator God; God is manifested as Redeemer God; God is manifested as Revealer God. Does it seem to you that most

Christians have equated God with Creator and have separated Jesus and Holy Spirit as distinct entities?

As a point of reference, consider that "monolatry" means the worship of only one God, while admitting the existence of other gods. "Monotheism" means the belief that only one God exists. Are you a monolatrist, or monotheistic, or a polyolatrist? A polyolatrist worships God as Father, and Jesus as God. There are two gods. That would be polyolatry.

What is the relationship between Jesus and God? Is Jesus God in human form? Some people use the language, and some talk at Christmas time about God leaving Heaven and "becoming flesh," God in-carnate. When God did that, did God leave any part of God behind in Heaven? If all of God moved over to Earth, did that vacate something over there in Heaven for the thirty years Jesus was alive on Earth?

These are such intense and meaningful questions that may have been ignored far too long because they are so difficult and complex. In order to clarify your faith, the questions have to be sorted. Once the questions are stated in understandable terms, then you can begin to resolve the issues and evolve some answers to a few of the problems of Trinity. As you work on this puzzle, you build your house of faith on a firmer foundation.

Do you believe that you can be a Christian and not be trinitarian? How do you connect the straw of the Doctrine of the Trinity with the clay of your experience? This is difficult and for many it's impossible. Martin Luther said that pondering the Doctrine of the Trinity drove him crazy. Thinking about Trinity can be a healthy thing for you when you think carefully about your concept of God, the attributes of God and how God relates to creation, redemption, revelation, wisdom, love, and many other essential activities.

11. IS IT NECESSARY TO BELIEVE IN THE TRINITY TO BE A CHRISTIAN?

A basic idea of this doctrine is "one in three, and three in one." The hymn says, "God in three persons, blessed Trinity." From your perspective, is there more emphasis on the One or on the Three, or is the emphasis about equal?

The biblical references to "three persons of the Godhead" are in a long discourse by Jesus in John 14-16, in a baptismal formula in Matthew 28:19, and in a benediction in II Corinthians 13:13. Do these three passages suffice to indicate that the Doctrine of the Trinity is biblically-based, as opposed to being of human invention?

Some scholars believe that the Doctrine of the Trinity is an attempt to reconcile Jewish Christians, with their strict belief in one God and one alone, with Gentile Christians, who needed Jesus to be the "Son of God," a separate deity of their contemporary time. Why do you think this may or may not be possible?

A basic idea of the Doctrine of the Trinity is that God reveals God equally as Creator (Father), Redeemer (Son), and Revealer (Holy Spirit). In other words, with equal emphasis, God is manifested as Creator, God is manifested as Redeemer, and God is manifested as Revealer. Does this work for you? Why or why not?

Does it seem to you that most people have equated God totally with Father, and separated Jesus Christ (and Holy Spirit) as a distinct entity?

Monolatry means the worship of only one God, while admitting the existence of other gods. Monotheism means the belief that only one God exists. Are you monolatrous? Are you monotheistic?

Do you believe that you can be a Christian and not be Trinitarian?

CHAPTER 12
IS THERE ONLY ONE CONCEPT OF THE WILL OF GOD?

There is more than one concept of the will of God. A dominant concept in the culture of the Western world (and in Islamic theology) is that God micromanages the universe. It is widely thought that unless you believe everything happens according to the will of God, you don't believe in God.

Because of this seemingly dominant concept of a micromanager God, when people say they don't believe in God, they're talking about the almighty, all-knowing God who determines, usually in advance, everything that happens. Anytime somebody says to you, "I don't believe in God," ask him or her to describe the God he or she doesn't believe in.

Margie sat down in the chair in my office and proclaimed, "I don't believe in God!"

I responded, "Describe for me the God you don't believe in."

"Are you trying to trick me," she said.

"No," I said. "You told me there is something or someone named 'God' that you don't believe in, so you obviously have a mental image of this person or thing that you don't believe exists, or that you don't want to exist. All I'm asking you to do is to describe that mental image."

She said, "Well, he's an old man with long white hair and a long white beard. He sits in a big chair behind a bar, like in a courtroom, and he's the judge of the world. He tells you what the punishment is for your sins. He doesn't smile much. He reminds me of a lot of preachers."

"And you don't like that judgmental God?" I asked.

"No, and I don't like the fact that he lets so many bad things happen that he could prevent if he wanted to, like famine and flood and disease and war," Margie said.

"So, that's the God you don't believe in?"

"Yes."

"Now, do me a favor," I said. "Describe for me a God you could believe in."

"Well, first off, it would be a loving God, who cared for everyone equally," she began. "This God would love me unconditionally, allow me to be free, and not condemn me when I make a mistake."

"Would you be able to feel a real sense of love for a God like that?" I asked.

"Sure," she responded.

I said, "Do I have some good news for you" . . .

Your understanding of God's will may be the most dynamic factor in your daily faith. If you don't believe that God micromanages the universe, there is a good chance you struggle with the majority's concept of the will of God, asking how God can let babies die of starvation, mothers die of cancer and fathers die in war, or you may have given up the struggle and declared yourself an atheist or agnostic.

The concepts of the will of God form a wide spectrum. Here in outline form are four sample concepts. There are many more.

The **Controller of the Universe** foreordained and predestined the smallest detail of daily life from the time of the creation of the world. God not only knows what you will do today, but causes it to happen. Fires, famine, pestilence and war all happen according to the will of God, though you may not be able to discern God's purpose. Love, marriage, jobs, houses, and children are all brought to you according to God's will. Ultimately, your salvation is determined by the will of God.

When Timothy McVeigh blew up the Murrah Federal Building in Oklahoma City, I was at home fifteen miles away. I didn't hear anything at 9:02, but I felt a thud of concussion on the side of the house and thought a car had missed the curve on the street and had run into the side of my house. Shortly thereafter I was standing beside District Attorney Bob Macy as it dawned on all of us the magnitude of this tragedy. Soon after that, I joined a group of volunteer chaplains in ministering to rescue workers who had seen more death and carnage than ever before in their experience. They were hugging trees and crying their eyes out. We took the place of the trees until we were ordered out of the area because of the second false bomb scare. After that time, they rescued one more person. They had to amputate her leg to get her out.

The next few days I spent with the families of those missing and presumed dead. There were many acts of kindness, but some thoughtless comments, as far as these people were concerned. A few people were saying that God miraculously preserved the survivors. The logical implication was that God didn't preserve those who died. It was heart-breaking to see an 8-year-old boy and his 6-year-old sister sitting alone in silence, holding hands, waiting for the news that both their parents had been killed in the blast.

This experience had a huge theological impact on Oklahoma City for the next few months. The concept of the will of God was on everybody's mind. Old belief bricks were thrown away and hauled off with the remnants of the Murrah Building. New belief bricks were made and put in place. A lot of people came to believe that God isn't the Controller of the Universe, that God doesn't will evil like this to happen, that evil acts can happen because of the bad choices of human beings. A lot of people refused to blame that bombing on God.

In the **Scriptwriter** scenario, God's will for your life is contained in a hidden script. God has written out how your life would be at its best. If you follow God's will for your life, life is so wonderful. Unfortunately, you do not have direct access to the script, so you must speculate a lot. You want to choose to live your life as God has scripted it, so you pray that God will reveal to you God's will for your life. If and when you manage to overlay the script with the decisions you make, life is wonderful indeed. Otherwise, it's the pits. If you get it overlaid, then it's good. If you don't, not so good.

As the **Freedom Lover**, God's will is for you to be a free and responsible human being, making your own decisions and handling the consequences. God loves you like the ultimate parent, willing to give you radical freedom. God rejoices with you when you make good decisions and doesn't interfere with your enjoyment of the good consequences. God shares your sadness when bad consequences follow bad decisions. God chooses not to know in advance what your decisions will be and chooses not to control your actions. God's will is God's wish that you live a joyful, peaceful existence.

In the role of **Clockmaker**, God created the Universe as a clockmaker makes a clock. God designed and built everything the way it was to be, according to God's will. Once everything was put together correctly, the Universe and everything in it was set in motion and God withdrew from the scene, leaving you completely on your own within God's created order. God's will is seen in the way things and people function naturally.

God as Clockmaker is the Deist point of view. Thomas Jefferson and Benjamin Franklin were both Deists. So was George Washington, and others of our founding fathers. A lot of intellectuals embrace the Clockmaker concept of the will of God. It connects with their clay.

The challenge is to find your place along the spectrum and write your own understanding of the will of God. This brick may change several times over your lifetime as your concept of God changes. But write your own concept of the will of God, and your own understanding, because every day you may ponder this matter of the will of God. This is an operative theological concept that you may work on and think about at least for five seconds every day. It's important for you to have a clear understanding for yourself of where you are in this matter of the will of God. It's very crucial and very critical.

Also, it's important to realize that you can move around on this spectrum. I'm most comfortable with the concept of God's will operating as Freedom Lover. That's where I function in my theology most days. But I've had some experiences in the Scriptwriter area, some very significant events in my life, where I felt like I really didn't have a choice. One example is my theology of "call."

> **When I was a teenager, I swore that I would never become the pastor of a church. I saw the negative things the church did to my father, including taking all his time, especially some time I wanted him to spend with me. So, I was happy being a French major in college instead of being a religion major. After college, my first job was teaching junior high girls French and Latin at The Westminster**

Schools in Atlanta. After two years of teaching, I went to graduate school at Vanderbilt University, hoping to get a Ph.D. in philosophy of religion and teach college undergraduates.

After three semesters of courses, it became apparent to me that college teaching wasn't in my future. I had met one of the best philosophers of religion and I couldn't even stand in his shadow. I'm not as analytical a thinker as you need to be to teach philosophy of religion. I put stuff together better than I take it apart.

For several months, I flopped around like a fish on a boat dock. Meanwhile, I had married and had told Donna that we would teach together for the rest of our lives. Now, I didn't know what I was going to do, but I knew I wasn't going to be a pastor. In fact, I was enjoying making fun of some of my classmates who were heading for pastoral ministry.

I reached the point where I had to make a career decision. I made a list of occupations I was interested in and/or had done and/or could be educated to do and/or had some natural ability to do. The list included teacher, counselor, politician, actor, singer, radio personality, youth worker, journalist, salesman, and public relations specialist. The next task was to put the list in priority order, and, bingo, I'd know what I was going to do. But, try as I did, I couldn't make that list give up its priorities.

Then, a holy moment happened! The pencil in my hand drew a circle around the whole list, and I knew that everything on the list was involved in one and only one occupation: pastoral ministry. It became very clear to me that the job I had sworn never to do was the job I had to do. It was the job I was suited for and had the ability to do in a good way. I protested with all my heart, but it didn't do any good. I entered the ministry, kicking and screaming. It turned out to be a good thing.

12. IS THERE ONLY ONE CONCEPT OF THE WILL OF GOD?

Read the four sample concepts below and see if any of these match up with the concept(s) you prefer most of the time.

A. Controller of the Universe

God's will is the controlling force of the Universe. Everything happens according to the will of God: the good, the bad, and the ugly. The smallest detail of daily life is foreordained and predestined by God from the time of the creation of the world. God not only knows what you will do today, but causes it to happen. Fires, famine, pestilence and war all happen according to the will of God, though you may not be able to discern God's purpose. Love, marriage, jobs, houses, and children are all brought to you according to God's will. Ultimately, your salvation is determined by the will of God.

B. Scriptwriter

God's will for your life is contained in a hidden script. God has written out how your life would be at its best. If you follow God's will for your life, life is so wonderful. Unfortunately, you do not have direct access to the script, so you must speculate a lot. You want to choose to live your life as God has scripted it, so you pray many prayers that God will reveal to you God's will for your life. If and when you manage to overlay the script with the decisions you make, life is wonderful indeed. Otherwise, it's the pits.

C. Freedom Lover

God's will is that you be a free and responsible human being, making your own decisions and reaping the consequences. God loves you like the ultimate parent, willing to give you radical freedom. God rejoices with you when you make good decisions and is sad with you when bad consequences follow bad decisions. God chooses not to know in advance what your decisions will be, and chooses not to control your actions. God's will is God's wish that you live a joyful, peaceful existence.

D. Clockmaker

God created the Universe as a clockmaker makes a clock. God designed and built everything the way it was to be, according to God's will. Once everything was put together correctly, the Universe and everything in it was set in motion and God withdrew from the scene, leaving you completely on your own within God's created order. God's will is seen in the way things and people function naturally.

Now write your own understanding of the will of God.

SECTION D
MIXING CLAY AND STRAW TO MOLD BELIEF BRICKS AND UNDERSTANDING HOW BELIEF BRICKS RELATE TO DAILY EXPERIENCES

Once you have begun to make belief bricks and construct your spiritual house of faith, it is exciting to see how faith works in practical matters. Practical issues must be dealt with one day at a time, and there should be integrity between what you believe and how you deal with the issues.

In Section C, we dealt with the difficult topics of the Bible, Jesus, Holy Spirit, Trinity, and the will of God. That's tough and very important doctrinal faith. This section is about practical faith with a little bit of the heady stuff mixed in. The issue at hand is application of belief to daily life, how and when and where "the rubber meets the road."

You probably think about some of these issues on a daily basis. Abortion, stem cell research, suicide, capital punishment, right/wrong, good/evil, war/peace, salvation, afterlife: these are massive issues we all confront as human beings. There should be integrity in your faith about these matters. You can have a reasoned argument for your position on these various matters, because they are all primarily matters of faith. For example, the abortion issue hinges on what you believe about the beginning of human life, conception or birth.

The reason you may disagree with another person on these matters is that your clay is different, and you may not have access to the same straw. Tolerance is a virtue when discussing tough issues.

> **When I was in Divinity School, John Fairweather was a student with me, and we disagreed on everything. We loved each other like brothers. We sometimes cut class to play ping pong. John is a Democrat, and I'm a Republican. John is from Iowa, and I'm a Son-of-the-South. John is Disciples of Christ. I grew up a Baptist. John majored in Ethics. I was in Old Testament studies.**
>
> **John and I argued about everything. We learned to disagree agreeably, and he taught me a great deal, because I listened to what he had to say. In order to refute him, I had to listen to him. That was great fun. Tolerance was a virtue.**

CHAPTER 13

WHAT IS HUMAN NATURE?
WHEN DOES HUMAN LIFE BEGIN AND END?

When someone begins considering the question, "Who is God?," a second question comes quickly, "What is human nature?" Is human nature evil, good, bad or neutral? What's the difference between human nature and human activity?

The story of Adam (Human Being) and Eve (Living Being) in the Garden of Eden (Fertility) is commonly understood to contain the story of the "Fall of Humankind." God tells the new people not to eat the fruit of the Tree of the Knowledge of Good and Bad. The "Devil" (a.k.a. serpent) tempts Eve to eat. She eats and gives some to Adam and they both have disobeyed God, incurred God's eternal wrath by their sin, and their human nature is sinfully evil and inherited by all humans. This is the Doctrine of Original Sin.

What you believe about human nature and the beginning of human life determines your position on abortion. What you believe about the sanctity of life determines what you believe about capital punishment and war. What you believe about the end of human life determines what you believe about euthanasia and suicide. What you believe about human nature is related to everything that has been said in this book so far.

The story of the Garden of Eden is the traditional source of the teaching that human nature is bad or evil. This story has been used to indicate that Adam and Eve sinned by eating the fruit of the forbidden tree, resulting in the fall of humankind, and that human nature has been sinful ever since.

This story may not be about human nature changing from good to evil. It may not be a story of original sin. It may be a story about God's giving people a chance to be human beings with opportunities to choose to do both good and bad.

Here is an alternative understanding of the creation stories in Genesis. You have a choice.

> There are two accounts of creation in Genesis, one which is actually a description and one which is a story. In both accounts, God created the world. The description in Genesis 1 says that after everything God created, God looked at it and said, "It's good." There is no verse in that description where God said, "It's bad." Every creature and every part of creation is said to be good.
>
> In the old story in Genesis 2-3, God created the animals and brought them to Adam for Adam to name. God created all the animals to serve and help Adam, including the serpent. Everything that was created was created to help Adam.
>
> The serpent was created to be a servant to Adam. What does the serpent do? The serpent cannot carry heavy loads like a horse. The serpent cannot help Adam by giving him

milk like a cow. What are we told about the serpent to describe his qualities to help Adam? One quality of the serpent is given in most translations as "crafty" or "subtle." The Hebrew word for "crafty" or "subtle" is the same word as "naked." I've never seen a naked person be subtle. I've never seen a crafty person be naked. The word really means "wise." So the verse really says, "the serpent was wiser than all the other beasts" (Genesis 3:1).

The serpent also had the ability to speak, which none of the other animals in the garden had. So, the serpent could speak, and the serpent was wiser than all the other animals. These are the two gifts the serpent had to help Adam.

God created this beautiful garden, and right in the dead center of this garden, he put the Tree of the Knowledge of Good and Bad. The story also tells us that next to this Tree of the Knowledge of Good and Bad was another tree, the Tree of Immortality.

Then God said to the two fifteen-minute-old people, "Don't eat from that tree there!" What does that mean in terms of the people that God created here, Adam and Eve? They didn't know good from bad. Did these people know that it was bad to disobey? No, they didn't know anything was bad. They didn't know that anything was good, either. They simply were told not to eat the fruit from a specific tree.

What did they do? First of all, Eve had a conversation with the serpent.

The serpent said, "Did God tell you not to eat of that tree?"

Eve said, "Yes. That's right."

The serpent said, "What would happen, if you ate from that tree?"

Eve said, "We'll die."

The serpent replied truthfully, "You won't die. Go ahead and eat!"

Now, what if that was what the serpent was created to do? Otherwise, he was going to have to follow these two people around the rest of their lives and tell them everything that's good and bad, because nobody else could talk to them except God.

So, he said, "Let's cut to the chase. Just eat from the tree! Eat from the tree, for crying out loud! And then, you'll know what's good and bad, and I won't have to follow you around the rest of my life!"

The serpent was created good for the purpose of helping Adam. Maybe there's some humor here. Maybe this is God saying, "I know how to get them to eat from that tree! I'll tell them not to."

There is a terrific song from a musical called *The Fantasticks*:

> Why do the kids put beans in their ears?
> Children can't hear with beans in their ears.
> Why do the kids put beans in their ears?
> They do it 'cause you say, NO!
> Why do the kids put jam on the cat ?
> Strawberry jam all over the cat . . .

You know that children never thought about putting jam on the cat 'til you said, "Don't put jam on the cat!" So why in the world would you tell fifteen-minute-old people, "Don't eat from that tree!" So, why did God put that Tree of the Knowledge of Good and Bad right smack dab in the middle of the garden and point to it? Why didn't God put it way over there on the edge of the garden and put a briar patch around it? If you don't want somebody to eat from a tree, why don't you hide the tree? Do you see what concept of God you have to buy into if you buy into the concept that this is the original sin? It's a concept of God who puts a tree right in the middle of a garden, points to it and says, "Don't touch that! If you do, I'll have to kill you!"

What if this is part of God's great master plan to make sure these people are going to be human beings, because they have to know the difference between good and evil before they can have freedom and responsibility, before they can be really human, because until that time they are puppets! Does God want puppets, or does God want to be loved freely? Is God the puppet master who controls people with strings, thus enslaving them and ensuring that people have to love God and obey out of duty and bondage?

The next section of the story portrays God's cursing of the serpent and Eve and Adam. Since these verses are written in poetic form and are found in the middle of prose narrative, many scholars maintain they were placed there by an editor with a particular agenda, many centuries later. So, if you omit these verses and continue reading the prose narrative, the text says that God gave Adam and Eve clothes. It doesn't say that God was angry. God just gave them clothes and said, "Out you go!"

God put them out the door, outside the gates of the Garden of Eden and put a guard there, the story says, to keep them from going back, to keep them away from the Tree of Immortality. Why didn't God tell them in the first place, "Don't eat from the Tree of Immortality?" He didn't say anything about that tree. Why not? What's the point of the old Storyteller? What if this story presents the Garden of Eden as a symbol of childhood and adolescence? What if being cast out of the Garden is symbolic of the natural process of moving into adulthood, with all its trials and tribulations, but also its freedom and responsibility? Maybe this is not the story of the Fall of Humankind nor the basis for the Doctrine of Original Sin

Is human nature essentially good or bad or neutral? Let's make a distinction between human nature and human activity. A river is a river is a river is a river. Is a river good or bad? It's just a river. A tree is a tree is a tree. Is a tree good or bad? It's just a tree. A human is a human is a human is a human. Is the human good or bad? The human is just a human. What about human activity?

If the river floods, is the river good or bad? It's just bad from your perspective if it hurts you, isn't it? If a tree falls on your car, that's a bad tree. If a human being chooses to do something bad, that's a bad human. That's a judgment call for you to make.

As you think about good activity and bad activity, you have to decide how much freedom you have to choose your own life. How much freedom do you think God has given you to choose your own life, to make your own decisions, for good or bad?

Have you done good things in your lifetime? Sure, you've done good things. Have you ever done anything sacrificial? Let's define sacrifice. Sacrifice means that you personally got nothing from doing a particular deed. This is pure altruism. If you get great pleasure and satisfaction from doing it, is it sacrifice? What if you get a blessing out of doing it, is that sacrifice or not?

Does it get back to intention? What if I do a good deed with the intention of getting something back, like recognition or fame or a good feeling in my heart? What if I don't go into it with any intention whatsoever to receive anything in return, but the satisfaction comes? The word "intention" comes in again. It's what you intend. Think about whether sacrifice has to be a burden. Is it possible for you to do something that you think is going to be a sacrifice, yet you are willing to do it? You're making a choice. Sacrifice could mean that you choose not to do one thing but choose to do another thing, not with the idea of getting anything out of it, but because you love a person or institution or ideal. In extreme situations, sacrifice could mean defeating one's own survival instinct to save the lives of others.

Sacrifice and evil are both rare, but they both exist. We humans do good and bad a lot. But evil, on the far side of the bad, and sacrifice, on the far side of the good, are rare commodities. I encourage you to think about those definitions. Does any of this straw touch your clay? Can you use any of this to make your own belief bricks?

WHEN DOES HUMAN LIFE BEGIN AND END?

Abortion, capital punishment, euthanasia, gene therapy, and cloning of human beings all beg the question of when human life begins and ends. These are considered to be some of the most controversial and difficult social issues of our lives and times. There have been and will be laws passed to deal with these issues, which means they are considered legal issues. Some of them have become political issues, and there are citizens who cast their votes for the candidate who espouses their side of the issue.

But these five issues are not primarily social, legal or political issues. First of all, they are issues of faith. Where you are on these issues is determined by what you believe, consciously or unconsciously, about human nature and human life.

The faith questions are critical. When does human life begin? How you answer that question determines where you are on abortion. Which is more important to you: the quality of life or the quantity of life? Is there life in a person when there is little or no memory or brain function? When does human life end? Your answers to these questions dictate your position on euthanasia, or mercy killing, or doctor-assisted suicide. Does the state have the right to take the life of a citizen of that country when that citizen has been convicted of a heinous crime? Is it right to destroy life, even life that was created in a petri dish, in order to save human lives? Is it right to create physically identical human beings?

Many people are not conscious that their positions on these issues are faith-based. They have never thought about where their social, legal or political passion, if they are passionate, came from. It begins with their concept of God and how and why God created and creates humans, if they believe God created and creates. It goes from there to whether they believe that every human being is endowed with an immortal soul or spirit, and if that soul or spirit is implanted at conception or birth. That has to be a part of a concept of human nature.

It is very important for you to know what you believe on these important issues, but even more important that you know WHY you believe what you believe. The WHY is an important clue to WHAT you really believe about the nature of God, as you understand God. If the militants in our society understood the WHY, there could be more patience with and tolerance of those who hold a different position. There are good people, decent people, spiritual people on all sides of these issues. They have just grabbed on to the elephant at different places.

> **Six blind people, standing side by side, were told by their sighted guide that there was an elephant standing peacefully in front of them in the clearing. None of these six people had ever encountered an elephant before. They all moved forward with hands outstretched and touched the elephant.**
>
> **The first grabbed the tail and said, "The elephant is a rope."**
>
> **The second reached around a leg and said, "The elephant is a tree."**
>
> **The third smacked into the side and said, "The elephant is a wall."**

> The fourth felt an ear and said, "The elephant is a big leaf."
>
> The fifth slid his hands along a tusk and said, "The elephant is a horn."
>
> The sixth was encircled by the trunk and cried, "The elephant is a great snake."
>
> They were then led away by their guide and disputed for months the nature of the elephant and never reached agreement. – **Author Unknown**

Each of the six was right and none was wrong. They could have grown and learned and gained much had they listened to one another and put together the bigger picture of the elephant. In their encounter with this big idea of "elephant," each knew only that part of the elephant each had touched and related it to something definite in past experience (clay).

How does this straw touch your clay? What are the unprocessed experiences that you can now process and use to mix with straw to make belief bricks?

13. WHAT IS HUMAN NATURE?
WHEN DOES HUMAN LIFE BEGIN AND END?

What is the difference, if any, between human nature and human activity?

Is human nature essentially good or bad or neutral? Why?

Do you believe that humans were created in the "image of God"? If so, what does that mean?

Do you believe that human life begins at conception or birth, or some other time? Why?

How much freedom do you have to choose your own physical and/or spiritual life?

Do you believe you have the freedom to terminate your own physical life?

How much responsibility are you willing to accept for your own life?

Who else are you responsible for at this point in your life?

CHAPTER 14
HOW DO YOU KNOW WHAT'S RIGHT AND WRONG?

If God is revealed to you in personal ways, and if you have the freedom to build your personal faith, you have to spend some time molding belief bricks dealing with the problem of right and wrong. You may need to reflect on the origin of your personal moral code.

This chapter seeks to tie your faith to fundamental ethical issues that you confront every day. You may need to wrestle with matters like lying, cheating, stealing, conscience, sin, guilt, forgiveness, individual vs. societal priorities, homosexuality, adultery and divorce. It's all about ethicality and morality. Let's see how all this impinges on your concept of God.

People say, "I know what's right and wrong by reading the Ten Commandments." If you look closely at the "Ten Commandments" you'll find that there are "Thirteen Words," not ten commandments. (The Hebrew noun translated "commandment" actually means "word.") From Jews to Roman Catholics/Protestants to the Eastern Orthodox Churches, all three groups claim a different ten out of that same thirteen. The Thirteen Words are:
1. I am YHWH your God.
2. Don't believe in the existence of any other gods.
3. Don't make idols or images of YHWH or any other gods.
4. Don't worship idols or images of YHWH or any other gods.
5. Don't use the name of YHWH in making a covenant and then break that covenant.
6. Remember to keep holy the seventh day of the week.
7. Honor your parents.
8. Don't murder.
9. Don't commit adultery.
10. Don't kidnap another person.
11. Don't lie in court.
12. Don't steal another person's real estate.
13. Don't steal another person's personal property.
    (Author's translation/paraphrase)

And furthermore, if you really want to count them, there are 613 commandments throughout Exodus, Leviticus, Numbers, and Deuteronomy, not thirteen. So, you're going to have to decide which ones of those you're going to obey and which ones you're not! For example, Leviticus 19:19 says, "You shall not breed your cattle with a different kind." That means that you shouldn't cross-breed your cattle. The second part of the verse is: "You shall not plant two different kinds of crops in the same field." That prohibits agricultural double-cropping. And number three: "You shall not wear a garment made of two different kinds of material." You may be wearing something with two different kinds of material right now, like a 60% cotton and 40% polyester garment.

Before judging the meaning of these "commandments," it is important to investigate whether they refer literally to animals, crops, or garments. This is true of other commandments, as well. The context and historical background are basic to interpreting and understanding these commandments in order that we don't misuse or abuse the biblical text. The purpose of the verse cited above is to emphasize the importance of racial purity. The point is the purity of the Hebrew people. The point of these three commandments is not what kind of clothes you're wearing. Pure animals, pure crops, and pure garments are symbolic of racial purity. It was important for the Hebrew writers to demonstrate that God was holy and had said that Israel was to be holy. This meant, among other things, that Israelites were not to behave in the same way, worship the same gods or believe like the people of neighboring countries. Rather, they were set apart, not for privilege but for responsibility.

Because of three insertions made very late in the editing of the first five books of the Bible (Exodus 34:28, Deuteronomy 4:13, Deuteronomy 10:4), people have always assumed that the "Ten Commandments" were written on the two stone tablets that Moses brought down from the top of the mountain where the tablets were inscribed by the hand of God. However, the biblical record (Exodus 24:7) says that the contents of the legal material was called the "Book of the Covenant." The original "Book of the Covenant" has forty-six (46) "commandments" in it (Exodus 20:22-23:19).

The Thirteen Words were originally a series of blessings and curses. Throughout the Hebrew Bible and New Testament, there is evidence of the importance of blessings and curses. In Deuteronomy 27:11-28:6 and in Joshua 8:30-35, you will find the Service of Blessings and Curses, the Annual Covenant Renewal Festival at Shechem, where the priests put half of the Hebrew tribes on the side of Mount Ebal and the other half on the side of Mount Gerizim. The priests would stand in the valley between them and would shout out blessings, and the tribes on Gerizim would cry out, "Amen." And the priests would shout out curses toward Mount Ebal, and those tribes would cry out, "Amen." They were witnesses against themselves, it says. The biblical text says that Moses laid this out for them, and Joshua had them do it to demonstrate that they were faithful to Yahweh.

Jesus was doing the same thing in the Sermon on the Mountainside in the fifth chapter of Matthew. The Beatitudes are blessings. Luke's version of this same sermon contains curses as well as blessings. Matthew didn't write the curses. Luke put them in. Jesus began the Sermon on the Mountainside with blessings and curses, just like they did at Shechem, because he was trying to get them back to the kind of spirituality Moses was promoting.

What you just read is straw, possibly new straw for you. It is a short history and explanation of the "Ten" Commandments. The detail was necessary because these commandments make up the basis of many people's moral code, but there are other sources that inform people about morality, such as the conscience.

What does your conscience tell you about what's right or wrong? Do all humans have a conscience that functions the same way and provides the same guidance? Are there a-moral humans who are without consciences?

What is sin? Who determines what is a sin? Is sin anything I do that you don't do, that you think is wrong? What is your definition of sin? Is sin the intentional hurting of God or another person? Are sin and evil the same thing?

Is there a difference between good guilt and bad guilt? How do you define them, if both exist? Is guilt good when it slows you down from repeating something bad you did and for which you were sorry? Is guilt bad when you let it eat you up, because you won't accept forgiveness for it? Is guilt bad when you let those feelings of guilt control you all your life and you die with it?

Is there anything you can do for which God will never forgive you? The Bible says God does not forgive blasphemy against Holy Spirit (Matthew 12:31), refusing to accept the great intangible gifts of God. What does Holy Spirit stand for? What is Sacred Breath of Life? Sacred Breath of Life is the first gift of God, symbolic of all the rest of the gifts of God. Blasphemy against Holy Spirit is refusing to accept the gifts of God, including the very gift of life itself, without which nothing else is possible. When you accept life as a gift of God, you can change. It is unforgivable only as long as you continue to deny God's gifts, because as long as you deny those gifts, you're spiritually dead. As long as you say, "I can do it on my own, God; I don't need anything from you in order to live my life as I think it ought to be lived," you're living an empty existence.

This raises the question of suicide, and there are at least two answers to that question. On the one hand, God has given everybody the freedom to terminate their own existence, and God forgives suicide. This answer is based on the concept that God is the perfect parent. A perfect parent would forgive his or her child who committed suicide. God would understand and forgive.

The other answer is "NO." God condemns those that commit suicide. It is a "mortal sin" and there is no salvation for one who kills oneself. What does your experience tell you about suicide?

This has a lot to do with spiritual death. I've been there, and I know that in spiritual death I was hurting so badly that I wanted to commit suicide. But I didn't think I deserved it. It was too good, too easy. Sometimes, in spiritual death it hurts so bad that people just kill themselves physically. Some people start drinking at that point and they just drown in it. They go alcoholic for the rest of their lives. Some people do drugs. All these are ways to escape the pain, but where is the life? Without hope, there is no quality of life.

Who determines what's right and what's wrong? If you had children and they were very hungry or starving, and you had no resources, would it be wrong to steal bread to feed them? This is the old situational ethics question. How do you see it? Is right or wrong a matter of individual priorities, in other words, "Okay, I'll decide for myself what's right or wrong," or is right and wrong determined by societal priorities?

On an island in the South Pacific, there was a native tribe that worshiped the most powerful force experienced by the people of that island, a volcano. It was their practice once a year to sacrifice a virgin by throwing her into the volcano to appease the volcano god. And so, for the good of the people and as a religious rite, they sacrificed a virgin, who was thrilled to have been chosen, to the volcano. It was right for them. Were they wrong?

In Egypt, from time to time, the idea was to throw babies into the Nile to the crocodiles who were considered to be embodiments of gods of the river. They were convinced that doing this kept the river from drying up or flooding too much at the wrong time in the growing season. Was that right or wrong? This practice was culturally based.

In India in years past, when the man died, his widow was burned on the same funeral bier as he was. Was that right or wrong?

To what extent is right or wrong a cultural, societal matter? You have to decide. There are things we do in the United States of America that are weird to a lot of people. We practice capital punishment. There are a lot of people around the world who look at this country and say, "Americans are dead wrong! You're barbaric!" That's another culture looking at our culture.

We have guns everywhere in this country. There are people in this world who think it's wrong for us to have such weapons of destruction and killing in every house in this country. Is it right or wrong? Do we just let our American culture determine what's right and wrong?

Whether you are guided by the Bible, your conscience, and/or the laws of your society, you have to answer for yourself the question, "How do I determine, how do I know what's right and wrong? Who or what tells me what's right and wrong? How do I know that?" Nobody can answer it for you, although many may try.

Does any of this straw touch your clay?

14. HOW DO YOU KNOW WHAT'S RIGHT AND WRONG?

Who and/or what tells you what's right and what's wrong?

How important to you are biblical teachings in determining what's right and wrong?

What does your conscience tell you about what's right and what's wrong?

What is sin?

What role should guilt play in your life? Is there good guilt and bad guilt?

Is there something you could do for which God would never forgive you? If yes, what?

If you had children and they were very hungry or starving and you had no resources, would it be wrong to steal bread to feed them? Why or why not?

Is right and wrong a matter of individual priorities? Why or why not?

Is right and wrong a matter of societal priorities? When some act is wrong in one society and right in another society, which society is right?

What do you believe about abortion, capital punishment, homosexuality, and how does that relate to your concept of God?

CHAPTER 15
CHAOS AND EVIL: DID THE DEVIL DO IT?

There are earthquakes, volcanoes, floods and hurricanes. Cancer, multiple sclerosis, and anti-immune diseases are a reality. Big airplanes blow out of the sky or crash into tall buildings and big ocean liners sink to the bottom. Good people suffer and die and we ask why. Is chaos in the world for a purpose or does it just happen? How does God relate to this discussion?

What is evil and where does it come from? In this chapter, you will find some of the common definitions of evil, leading you to ask the central questions that spiritual people ponder about the nature of evil. For instance, what causes human beings to do evil? Was evil created by God? Have you ever been evil? How is evil different from bad? Do you believe in a personal Devil or is that character a symbol of temptation or evil?

Did you know that:

- Most of what American Christianity believes about the Devil comes from Dante's *Inferno* and Milton's *Paradise Lost*, not from the Bible?

- Nowhere in the Bible do the words "Devil" and "Hell" occur in the same sentence?

- The word Satan is a Persian word, originally?

- Satan, transliterated from Persian into Hebrew, means "the Tempter"?

- Satan and the "Anger of the Lord" are used to mean the same thing in one repeated passage in the Hebrew Bible (II Samuel 24:1 and I Chronicles 21:1)?

- In the Prologue of Job, Satan shows up in the heavenly court of the Lord, along with the other "sons of God" *(b'nai elohim)*?

- In the gospel accounts of the temptation of Jesus, Mark refers to Satan, Luke to "the Devil" and Matthew refers to "the Devil," "the Tempter," and Satan?

The "Devil" has a history. There was no concept of a devil as an adversary of God in ancient Hebrew thought. Prior to 500 BCE, there was no concept of an adversary of God in any major religion in the world. In Hebrew thought, God is one and there is no other immortal being with superhuman powers (read "god") permitted.

As you read earlier, Zoroaster taught that everything was split into two, a thoroughgoing dualism. Until around 550 BCE, all religions had taught that all reality came together into the One. But Zoroaster said that there was a good god, named Ahura Mazda, and a bad god, named Angra Mainyu. Both of these gods had six lieutenants: Mithras was one on the good side, and Satan was one on the bad side. Mithras was a human-divine savior figure, and Satan was the embodiment of temptation. In addition, the good side had legions of angels and the bad side had hordes of devils or demons.

The idea was that there is a constant, cosmic battle going on between the forces of good and the forces of evil. This idea caught the imagination of the people of the Middle East, particularly after Persia under Cyrus the Great conquered the Fertile Crescent in the last half of the sixth century BCE. The Jews in captivity in Babylon were freed by Cyrus to go back to Jerusalem in 539 BCE. Hebrew thought was seriously affected by Zoroastrianism, as we see, for example, in the prologue to the book of Job where Satan is pictured as God's prosecuting attorney, roaming the earth and reporting on who is naughty and nice.

By the time of Jesus, Persian thought had been brought into Greek thought by way of Gnosticism. When the New Testament was written, Greek thought forms and Hebrew thought forms were competing for priority. In Matthew, Hebrew thought forms win by a slight majority, but in Mark, Luke, John, and the writings of Paul, Greek thought is predominant. Revelation is especially Greek in thought and is the main source of "information" about the Devil.

There are a few important questions to deal with relative to the Devil. Was evil created by God in the beginning or did God only create the potential for evil? Do you believe literally in the "evil one," also known as Devil, Satan, Lucifer, Beelzebub or Beelzebul? If so, is this being the source of all evil? If you believe literally in the Devil, do you see the Devil as an evil God?

People have asked me, "Can I have a third category other than human or divine?" If you want one, you can have one. Conventional wisdom is that every personal being is either human or divine. If you see angels as being actual, factual angels, and you've experienced that, no one can deny it. So, you'll have to make yourself a third category, unless you want to put angels and demons and devils in the god category. At this point, you have to admit that you're polytheistic and then say, "I don't believe in one God."

Do you believe there's a constant cosmic battle taking place between the forces of good and the forces of evil? The followers of Zoroaster have believed that for over 2,500 years. The Jewish sect known as Essenes believed that there would be such a battle one day. Many Christians, influenced by the book of Revelation and so-called "Bible prophets," believe in a final battle between the army of Christ and the army of the Anti-Christ, and they call it "the Battle of Armageddon." They believe it will signal the end of the world.

Let me give you an option on that one. The option is that this battle may be universal or final in the sense that it happens to every individual. My Battle of Armageddon was fought within me. I believe the Battle of Armageddon is fought within the hearts of every human being. That's what makes it universal. Because this is so universally individualistic, it's cosmic.

I had a dream of how that battle took place, and in that vision, I'm a knight in armor, sitting on a horse. I'm ready for battle, and I look up and there are 100,000 knights on horses across the field. They're my enemy. I know this is a hopeless battle, but I have to fight the battle. So, I charge. Instead of waiting for them to come to me and wipe me out, I charge to my certain defeat and death. As I get near them, they turn and run. All 100,000. Watching them flee, I rein up my horse. I feel a presence over my shoulder, and I turn around. Behind me, on a gigantic horse, is my huge God.

It reminds me of that scene in the movie, *The Bear*, in which the bear cub is being chased by the cougar. The cougar's going to kill that cub. He keeps stalking it, and the bear cub goes out on a tree that's fallen in the river. The bear cub keeps going and the cougar keeps following. When the bear cub gets as far out on the tree as he can go, when he can't go any further, just as an act of defiance, he rears up on his hind legs and roars as loudly as he can. And the cougar turns and runs. Then, the camera pans back, and right behind the cub is the mother grizzly bear, standing on her hind legs, nine feet tall. That's why that cougar cut the chase and ran.

That's what I saw behind me, except 'twas God on a horse! And I knew why the 100,000 had fled. But the other thing I noticed as I got close to them was the face of all those knights. Their faces looked exactly like my face!

I think each of us has to fight that battle. I personally don't have a concept of a cosmic Battle of Armageddon between the forces of good and evil. I've seen it. I've been in it. And it took place in my heart. There is the problem of the difference between bad and evil. Let's distinguish between bad and evil. For example, somebody is driving down the street and gets distracted and hits another car and someone is injured. That's bad, isn't it? Is it evil?

Timothy McVeigh made up his mind that he was going to get even with the federal government for what they did at Waco to the Branch Davidians. He blew up the Murrah Building in Oklahoma City and killed babies and innocent women and men. That's evil. Why is it evil? Because he deliberately intended to do it. Deliberate intention has to be a key part of the definition of evil.

Al-Qaeda and Usama bin Laden are committed to terrorist acts around the world. As I was writing this, some members of *al-Qaeda* crashed commercial airliners into the World Trade Center and the Pentagon, killing over 3,000 civilians and some military personnel. It was a despicable act of evil, carried out with the intention of killing innocent people and terrorizing a nation.

Have you ever done evil? Have you ever hurt another person, emotionally or physically, other than in a declared war, with malice aforethought, deliberately intending to hurt that person? An easier question is: have you ever done bad? Oh, yeah! We all know what bad is! Evil is a harder question, isn't it? "The Devil made me do it!" some people say. "I couldn't help it!" Yeah, they plead temporary insanity, right!

How does your concept of evil fit with your concept of God? Bad things happen to us when people make decisions that affect us negatively. Bad things happen to us when we make bad decisions. Bad things happen to us when chaos exists in nature. Is chaos caused by God or is chaos simply a matter of randomness? Is there randomness in the universe? Does your concept of God allow for randomness? That is to say, does God direct every tornado, every hurricane? Does God micromanage the universe or not? Does God cause every earthquake that happens? Does God cause every mud slide in Italy? Does God cause these catastrophes that take place? Is there chaos built within the universe, because we need chaos in order to be able to recognize order, or because chaos and order are both integral for the functioning of the universe? Is cancer caused by God, or is cancer caused by the chaotic division of cells? Is chaos a part of life and a part of the universe and a part of the will of God, as you understand the will of God?

Are you willing to accept the notion of chaos in your theology, or is that too threatening? It can be very threatening! Yet, chaos is a major faith issue, especially if it is experienced in the context of how you view good and bad and evil.

If you're going to be close to God, you're going to experience change because there's lots of change involved in being close to God. What happened to Moses when he got close to God on the mountain? He had to make a big change. Being close to God involves change if you believe God is dynamic. Moses' experience of the burning bush (Exodus 3) is an example of feeling God's presence at close range and being challenged to do what you never wanted or expected to do. That's a proto-typical worship service! If you attend a worship service, you ought to go in and take your shoes off, like Moses did, and expect to be challenged.

These are big faith issues worthy of the time you should spend considering them. Use the straw and process the clay to make belief bricks that you can use on a daily basis as you exercise your conscious faith.

15. CHAOS AND EVIL: DID THE DEVIL DO IT?

How do you define "evil"? How do you define "bad"? What's the difference?

Was evil created by God in the beginning, or did God only create the potential for evil?

Do you believe literally in The Evil One, a.k.a. Devil, Satan, Lucifer, Beelzebub? If so, is this person the source of all evil?

If you believe literally in the Devil, do you see the Devil as an evil god? If not, why not?

Do you believe there is a constant cosmic battle taking place between the forces of Good and the forces of Evil? If so, describe the battle.

How does your concept of evil fit in with your concept of the will of God?

What causes human beings to do evil?

Have you ever been evil? If so, what did you do that was evil?

What do you consider to be the most evil thing ever done by a human being or a group of human beings?

CHAPTER 16

ARE YOU SAVED?
WHERE DID HEAVEN AND HELL GO?
IS THERE GOING TO BE A JUDGMENT DAY?
WHERE DO YOU GO FROM HERE?

> Heaven is where the chefs are French,
> the police are British,
> the mechanics are German,
> the lovers are Italian,
> and it's all organized by the Swiss.
>
> Hell is where the chefs are British,
> the police are German,
> the mechanics are French,
> the lovers are Swiss,
> and it's all organized by the Italians.
> (Author unknown)

ARE YOU SAVED?

Salvation is a haunting and daunting issue for many people. For some, salvation is only in the future. After you die, you hope to "go to Heaven," and this life is preparation for that life. For others, salvation is here and now and "the Kingdom of God (or Heaven) is in the middle of you" (Luke 17:21). In this chapter, the task is to come to a clearer understanding of what you believe on these subjects concerning the hereafter, which have been of great motivational value to the Church through the ages.

A large percentage of Protestant Christians in America believes that "being saved" happens like this:

1. You are convicted of your sins. You become convinced that you have done so many bad things in your life that you have become unacceptable to God, and if you were to die physically right now, you would go straight to Hell.
2. You confess all your sins to God, acknowledge your unworthiness and ask forgiveness. If you confess honestly and fervently intend never to commit those sins again, God grants forgiveness.
3. You walk down the aisle during the invitational hymn or altar call and say aloud that you believe Jesus died on the cross for you and rose from the dead on the third day to be your Lord and Savior.
4. You are baptized with water, preferably immersed. (Some Christians believe that baptism alone is what saves you.) After initiation by baptism, you are a member of Jesus' Church. Now, you are saved and a Christian.

The above is an easy, commercial approach to salvation which, at best, may get a person started on the road to salvation, like a starting gun at the beginning of the race. At worst, this approach has turned many people away from Christianity forever because of a lack of substantive theology. This approach is centered on one emotional experience, the "day I was saved." It ignores the biblical record of the salvation process, such as Paul's injunction in Philippians 2:12 to "work out your own salvation with fear and trembling."

For the majority Christian, you are saved **from** eternal damnation in Hell with the Devil, and you are saved **to** eternal life in Heaven with God. The problem is that salvation becomes completely future-oriented, and life today takes on secondary significance. This position is in contrast with many biblical passages, such as Jesus' teaching in Matthew 6:34, which says, "Don't worry about tomorrow, for tomorrow will bring worries of its own. Today's trouble is enough for today."

Working out your own salvation is a daily process in which you and God are partners. An often-asked question among fundamentalist Christians is, "Are you saved?" The more important question may be, "Will you live this day in the presence of God?" Life lived in the presence of God IS Heaven, today and tomorrow. Life lived outside the presence of God IS Hell, today and tomorrow. There's some straw. Does it touch your clay?

WHERE DID HEAVEN AND HELL GO?

However, since most Christians believe you are saved from Hell to Heaven, it raises the question of the location of Heaven and Hell. Hell has always been "down there" and Heaven has always been "up there." In the 20th century, the geographical locations of Heaven and Hell were lost. Geophysicists didn't find Hell in the center of the planet, and pilots like Chuck Yeager couldn't locate Heaven above the clouds in the X-series rocket ships. Yet, Heaven remains "up there" and Hell is still "down there," illustrating the compelling power of unconscious faith.

My father had a great ministry in the Southern Baptist Convention. He served very successfully as pastor of four churches in Louisiana, Mississippi, and Tennessee in the 40's and 50's. He made very few mistakes in his ministry, but three of them got him blacklisted by the Baptists.

In 1954, Daddy decided he didn't know everything he wanted to know about the New Testament, and he wanted to go back to graduate school and get a Ph.D. His first mistake was to admit, as a Baptist pastor, that he didn't know everything there was to know about the New Testament. Furthermore, he decided that the best New Testament faculty in the world at that time was at the New College (theological graduate school) of the University of Edinburgh, Scotland, and not at one of the Baptist seminaries.

Off to Scotland the family went, for two years. My father immersed himself in Karl Barth and became a neo-orthodox theologian. On returning to the States, he accepted a call as pastor of First Baptist Church of Jefferson City, Tennessee, home of Carson-Newman College, a fundamentalist Southern Baptist school. In 1955, students and faculty alike

had burned copies of the Revised Standard Version of the Bible in a bonfire in the middle of the street, claiming that this translation by an outstanding committee of American scholars was the work of the Devil.

For five years, Daddy watched the theology in his sermons, very carefully skirting around the many controversial issues of Baptist faith, avoiding the elephant traps. The chair of the Board of Deacons of the church slept through every sermon every Sunday and would have slept through what he believed to be the Second Coming. One Sunday morning, Daddy made his third mistake. He decided he had been there long enough to be trusted to share just a little of the theology he picked up across the big pond. The chair of the Board of Deacons woke up just in time to hear Daddy preach that Hell might not be a geographical place but an experience of the absence of God in one's life.

Monday morning, my father found out Hell was a geographical place. It was Jefferson City, Tennessee, and he was smack dab in the middle of it. He resigned two weeks later.

Given the different meanings of the nature of Heaven and Hell and the various interpretations of the location of Heaven and Hell, you may be drawn to the biblical phrases, "Kingdom of Heaven" and "Kingdom of God." Matthew speaks of the "Kingdom of Heaven" where Mark seems to speak of the "Empire of God" and Luke and John speak of the "Kingdom of God." It is difficult to tell if the three phrases meant the same or something different to the early Christians in different places. The word "Kingdom" again raises the problem of location.

Where is the Kingdom? What does it mean when Jesus says, "The Kingdom is in the midst of you?" It means the Kingdom is here. The Kingdom is in us. But some people say that the Kingdom is up above the clouds. If so, then the Kingdom of Heaven is the same as the place of afterlife known as Heaven...up there, out there. Having asked the question of the whereabouts, then you can ask the question of when.

Some people say the Kingdom began at the time of Jesus' birth. Some say the Kingdom began at the time of Jesus' baptism. Some people say the Kingdom began at the time of Jesus' resurrection. Some people say the Kingdom began at Pentecost, fifty days after Easter. Some people say that the Kingdom isn't going to begin until the end of the world, which they say was supposed to have happened at the beginning of the third millennium, i.e. 2000 CE. This date of 2000 CE as the year of the end of the world is based on the idea that Jesus was born in 1 CE. Most scholars are in agreement that Jesus was born in 6 BCE, so the third millennium began in 1994. Both these years have already passed, and the world is still here.

The most commonly taught Christian position is that the Kingdom IS only in the future, after the end of the world, after the judgment. Only then comes the Kingdom. In other words, the world awaits the "Second Coming of Christ" for Jesus to straighten out this mess, bring down the new Jerusalem, and work it out where the lion will literally lie down with the lamb.

When is the Kingdom? The Kingdom can be here and now. The preponderance of statements credited to Jesus in the gospels say the Kingdom is here and now. He says that over and over. When he talks about the Kingdom, he says, "Don't go looking over yonder for the Kingdom. The Kingdom of Heaven is in the midst of you." If Jesus was the Messiah anticipated in the Hebrew Bible, then he was the one to inaugurate the rule and Kingdom of God on Earth. If Jesus was the Prince of Peace on whose shoulder the government of the Kingdom of Heaven would rest, then the Kingdom began some time during the life, ministry, death or resurrection of Jesus, and it continues today, unless you don't think Jesus did the job he was supposed to do.

Why is there a Kingdom of Heaven? Is it because God wants to share time with you, giving you continuing opportunity to be in the presence of God? Is it because it's your reward for a life well lived? There are many other possibilities.

Are there rules to follow in the Kingdom? If the Kingdom is here and now or the Kingdom is there and then, or the Kingdom is both, are there rules to follow in the Kingdom? Does the Kingdom have a king? If so, is it the Kingdom of God or the Kingdom of Jesus? Or is it God in Jesus? God manifested in Jesus?

Once in the Kingdom in the here and now, do you ever leave or can you be thrown out? If you are thrown out, can you get back in? Is there a revolving door?

This matter of the Kingdom of Heaven is a daily deal. Whether or not I am in the Kingdom today depends on whether I'm working on my covenant with God today. There are days when I don't live in the Kingdom. There are days when I do live in the Kingdom. Similarly, there are days when I'm a husband and there are days when I'm not a husband. The difference is, I'm either working on my covenant with my wife, or I'm not working on my covenant with my wife. Sometimes I'm in absolute dead neutral, got my motor in idle. I have an overall long-term commitment, but right now I'm not doing anything about it. So, I don't deserve to be called "married" or "Kingdom-ite." I quit trying to earn my salvation with righteous living because that idea had me totally intimidated. I died doing that. I died spiritually trying to get into that future salvation thing. I have to work on my salvation every day. I'm a work in progress. Consequently, there are days when I'm saved and there are days when I'm not saved. I believe God loves me even when I'm having a bad day, but at the same time, what good does that do as far as I'm concerned on that particular day? I'm still having a lousy day.

I really don't want to spend any more time worrying about future salvation. I have to worry about the present. I have all I can do to worry about salvation right now. My hands are full. I don't have the ability to do anything about the future. I'm going to trust God with the future.

One of the things that irritates me about the so-called "Bible prophets" (and there are a lot of "Bible prophets" out there today) is that "Bible prophecy" is an attempt at future-telling, which is totally contrary to everything in the Hebrew Bible. The Hebrew prophets were concerned with social injustices and misplaced worship in their own day, among other things. In the New Testament, the book of Revelation is used by soothsayers to predict the future when in truth it speaks only to the situation in the Roman Empire in the second century CE. I'm totally willing for God to be the God of the future. The future doesn't belong to me, but I do have some responsibility to plan for the future. When I need to know what's going to happen in the future, isn't that my lack of faith in God?

I can't control a thing other than right now. God gave me right now, and I'd better do a good job right now, because that's the only thing I can do anything about. I find that if I concentrate on the present, I do a lot better than if I concentrate on the future. If I concentrate on the future and neglect the present, I do badly.

I was teaching at The Westminster Schools in Atlanta, Georgia, and a Friday chapel speaker came in and told the kids that life is about preparing for the life hereafter and learning how to die, so that when you die, you can go to heaven. I had a theological problem with that then and still do.

IS THERE GOING TO BE A JUDGMENT DAY?

Do you believe in a Judgment Day at the end of time? If so, what happens then? If you don't believe in a Judgment Day and/or the end of time, why not? Michelangelo painted the picture of Judgment Day on the end wall of the Sistine Chapel of the Vatican in Rome. Some of the people in the picture are going up and some of them are going down. Jesus is standing in the middle. Some speak of this as the sheep going up to Heaven and the goats going to Hell. This celebrated piece of art has had a profound impact on the Christian understanding of Judgment Day as described in Matthew 25.

Long before Michelangelo painted that picture on that wall, there was a great debate about Judgment Day. The debate continues today, often with the added problem of the situation of the soul after death. When someone dies, does that person's soul go into a holding tank of souls, or directly to Heaven or Hell, depending on whether or not he or she was "saved"? Does there have to be a Judgment Day before you can have Heaven and Hell? If so, there's a whole lot of souls in the holding tank.

Some early Christians said that there was a holding tank which served as the place where people were purified after death. Origen, a brilliant Christian writer from the first half of the third century, is reported to have said that people were sent back to life on Earth to get it right the second time if they didn't get it right the first time, because they still had time until the "Second Coming" and before the eventual "Judgment Day" to get it right. There was a little bit of reincarnation involved in Origen's teaching.

Here's a classic example of a theological conundrum. Ralph is looking forward with great fervor to the "Second Coming of Christ" and the judgment of all souls over which Jesus is supposed to preside. After the judgment, the good souls, the "sheep," will go to Heaven to live eternally with God and Jesus. The souls judged by Jesus to be bad, the "goats," will go to Hell to burn eternally in the flames of the "Lake of Fire," presided over by the Devil and his hordes of demons.

At the same time, Ralph's mother, Alice, recently died. She was a good Christian woman, a faithful church member who "loved the Lord" and served him faithfully. She had been "saved" when she was fourteen years old. Ralph cannot imagine his mother's soul being stuck in a holding tank with billions of other souls, some of whom are very unsavory characters, like Adolf Hitler, Attila the Hun, and Queen Jezebel. Therefore, he believes that immediately upon her death, his mother rested safely "in the bosom of her Lord."

The problem is that Ralph can't have it both ways. These two positions are in direct conflict with one another. Ralph has to decide one way or another, unless he can come up with a new third position, which would be very creative.

This traditional belief in Judgment Day/End of the World is seen in burial practices. Most people are buried with their feet toward the east and their heads towards the west. Pastors are taught in seminary and divinity school always to stand at the west end of the casket when doing the interment service because that's where the head is in traditional cemeteries. We do that because of the unconscious faith that on "Resurrection Day" or "Judgment Day" or the "End of the World," all the dead people's bodies are going to be reconstituted in some mysterious way, all the dirt will fly off their graves, their casket lids will unlock and open, and without moving their feet, their bodies will angle up ninety degrees and be facing Jerusalem. Go to an old cemetery and check out the positions of the graves. But the question is, "When do the souls and bodies reconnect?" or do they?

WHERE DO YOU GO FROM HERE?

Do you believe in a physical, material, geographical Heaven and/or Hell in the life hereafter? If so, describe it or them. If not, what do you believe about life with or without God hereafter?

> What if, in the last life, we didn't have any mass? What if we were all energy? Energy and mass are the only two things that exist in the universe, and mass is maybe only the visible confluence of energy, anyway. What if we were all energy in the last life and we lived our lives there and tried to be good and we tried to believe, and God promised us that if we did that right, in the next life we could have mass? So, we went along, and we did it, and life was good. And then we died, however that happens to energy beings, and we were reborn into this life as energy with mass. For this seventy, eighty years, we get to enjoy the pleasures and endure the pains of mass on this planet, before we go back to being energy without mass in the next life. What if this life is the heaven we were promised in the last life? What if we yearned in the last life to be able to eat food and drink beverages and sleep and make love and play golf and walk in the sunlight? Many people are sitting here saying, "This life isn't good. The next life is gonna be better." Well, what if this is the "better" that we were promised last time? That's some very different straw!

What happens to your physical body when you die? There are those who say, "Well, the physical body is gone." There are those who say that the physical body will be re-constituted, kind of like instant coffee. You pour hot water and the ashes are reconstituted. There are others who say that miraculously the human body comes back together again, rearranged a little bit. There are different concepts and theologies about the human body after death. Where are you on this subject?

You have to look your mortality right in the eye and say, "Here's what I hope for in the next life." "Faith is the substance of things hoped for, the essence of things not seen" (Hebrews 11:1). What do you hope for after physical death? A small experiment has demonstrated that most people hope for the same thing in the next life that they hope for in this life, indicating that most of us see the next life as an extension of the hopes and dreams of this life.

Matters of salvation, Heaven, Hell, Kingdom of God, Judgment Day and afterlife are big issues for your faith, and they are all connected with your concept of the nature of God. The questions raised in this chapter, like all other questions in this book, are weighty and thought-provoking.

Does this material touch your clay? How? Why? Why not?

16. ARE YOU SAVED?
WHERE DID HEAVEN AND HELL GO?
IS THERE GOING TO BE A JUDGMENT DAY?
WHERE DO YOU GO FROM HERE?

How do you define "salvation?" "Saved" from what to what?

Where and when is the Kingdom of Heaven?

Who is (or will be) in the Kingdom of Heaven, and why is there (or will there be) a Kingdom?

Once in the Kingdom, do you ever leave or can you be thrown out? Can you get back in?

Do you believe in a physical, material, or geographical Heaven in the life hereafter? If so, describe it. If not, what do you believe about life with God hereafter?

Do you believe in a physical, material, or geographical Hell in the life hereafter? If so, describe it. If not, what do you believe about life without God hereafter?

Does one go immediately to heaven or hell when one dies or is there a holding tank? Is that Purgatory? What is the waiting for?

Is your entire life's purpose based on the life hereafter? If so, explain. If not, what is it based on?

Do you believe in a Judgment Day at the end of time? If so, what happens then? If not, why not?

What happens to your physical body when you die? On Judgment Day?

CHAPTER 17

DEPRESSION, DESPAIR, MID-LIFE CRISIS, THE DEATH OF THE HUMAN SPIRIT: IS THAT A SPIRITUAL EVENT?

This chapter may have the most impact of any in this book. More adults of forty-plus years will identify with this concept than any other I have presented. The point of this chapter is to demonstrate the spiritual nature of depression, despair and mid-life crisis. This is a chapter of new straw.

Everyone experiences spiritual death, sooner or later, except for those people whose physical life is snuffed out suddenly, before they encounter this universal phenomenon. Spiritual death can be defined as the experience of despair, when one feels the absence of God, confronts one's own mortality in a profound way and feels that life is meaningless and without purpose. This experience may be brief or may last for years. You may go slowly into the "dark night of the soul" or you may fall off the cliff into the bottomless pit. For many, if not most, the experience of spiritual death is directly related to the person's profound encounter with physical death. This happens when you really, REALLY understand that one of these days you're going to die physically, and you begin to ask serious questions about the meaning and purpose of life and questions about the nature of God.

Karen turns forty and her life is going down the drain. Instead of "life begins at forty," it's over. Her identity has been as wife and mother of two. Her husband is now married to his career. The youngest child is almost ready to call her blessed and leave the nest forever. She has lost her identity and her reason for being. It's the death of her human spirit.

When Josh was twenty and a senior in college, he was a compulsive moralist. His goal was to be ethically pure. He didn't drink, smoke, or curse. He didn't lie, cheat, or steal. He didn't date, dance with, or even swim with girls for fear of immoral thoughts. One day he discovered that he was trying to earn his salvation, and it wasn't working. He was miserable. Life was lousy. There was no meaning. He was hurting so much he wished he were dead. He was, spiritually.

Josh's spirit died over several years. When the finale came, he felt totally vacated in spirit and void in faith. Josh lost God, hope, and heaven. He felt that he was lying paralyzed on a beach, hands and arms outstretched, facing the sun, waiting to die. During this crucial moment, he considered suicide. The idea of ending it all was a welcome thought. He dismissed the idea because it was too easy and he didn't deserve anything that good.

> Sam is experiencing mid-life crisis. He hates his job, so he changes vocations. He hates his wife, so he divorces her and marries a younger woman. He hates the city in which he lives, so he moves to another. He hates himself for all the stupid decisions he has made in his life. He doesn't care anymore whether he lives or dies. Momentary pleasure is the key to his physical life. His human spirit is dead, and there is no more trying.

The human race is divided into three categories in this matter of spiritual death and resurrection. First, there is the "spiritual innocent" who has not yet experienced spiritual death. Obviously, the young fall into this category, but circumstances may keep you "innocent" until you are well up in years. I know people who are 75-years-old who are "spiritual innocents." There's no time frame on this.

Secondly, there is the "spiritually dead" whose spirit died yesterday or months or years ago and who is beginning the struggle to find new life, or who has resigned from life with no hope of ever knowing a purpose. This is the spiritual zombie. Your heart pumps inside your chest. You breathe in and out. You have a pulse. You go to work almost every day. But your eyes are vacant and your days are empty, and you are at least tempted to mask the pain with an addiction or end it all. What psychologists refer to as "mid-life crisis" is often spiritual death.

Thirdly, there is the "spiritually resurrecting" and "spiritually alive" segment of the population. You are struggling like mad to break out of the cocoon, or you have broken out as the butterfly, changed forever from the caterpillar. You have a new understanding of life, a new understanding of self, and a new understanding of God. Some people never make it to this stage.

Spiritual death is when you decide to quit your job, change vocations, divorce your spouse, and move to a new town. Oh, and get a new sports car. You woke up and looked at yourself in the mirror and saw a corpse and you decided, "this ain't working." You tried to run as hard as you could, and you couldn't get away from it, because it was inside you. So, you died spiritually. Sometimes, you stay dead.

The dominant theme of great literature, music, and motion pictures, of all the great classics of all civilizations on this planet during all of recorded history is spiritual death and spiritual resurrection. The authors, composers and directors don't use those terms, but that's what they present in their works. Look at all the main characters and events of the Bible.

> Paul of Tarsus was traveling from Jerusalem to Damascus with warrants to arrest Syrian Christians when he had an experience of the risen Jesus. Everything he had lived for up to that moment came to an end. His old spirit died. Peter of Bethsaida left his wife and children and his fishing business to be chief supporter of his good friend, Jesus. He poured his heart into the effort and it provided him with great meaning for his life. But after Jesus was arrested, he was afraid and told the people at the high priest's house that he'd never

known Jesus. When the rooster crowed that morning, and Jesus was crucified, Peter died spiritually.

Jeremiah was scheduled to die physically in the mud in the bottom of a dry cistern in Jerusalem. In the midst of the mud and the muck, he experienced the absence of God and died spiritually. Jacob knew Esau was going to kill him beside the Brook Jabbok, and he died spiritually. The story in Genesis tells that God told Abraham to take his only son, Isaac, up on the mountain and slit his throat and burn his young body, and Abraham died spiritually.

There are so many stories. You look through the Bible and you'll see pictures of spiritual death. They're everywhere. Each of the world's major religions deals with this theme in its own way. For example, a Buddhist seeks enlightenment to overcome spiritual death and live in harmony in the world and within the self by learning how to live in the midst of suffering and joy. A Muslim tries to conquer spiritual death by submitting completely to the will of Allah.

The enormous impact that Jesus has had on the people of this planet over the course of 2,000 years is due, in part, to the media coverage given his spiritual death, which happened simultaneously with his physical death. Biblical writers used the images of Good Friday to make Jesus into God's most profound symbol of the universal reality of spiritual death. In the picture of the crucifixion, there is the face of a person who is confronting his physical mortality, while at the same time expressing his feeling of the absence of hope and purpose and the absence of God.

The Greek used in the gospel accounts of the crucifixion says that Jesus "yelled at the top of his lungs" verses from a psalm entitled "My God, My God, Why Have You Forsaken Me?" Today, this is called the 22nd Psalm. Clearly, this is a verbal expression of spiritual death by Jesus. He felt that everything he had trusted in before was gone. He felt abandoned by God and overwhelmed by hopelessness. A sense of profound emptiness had seized him in the midst of his physical death in a rock quarry in Jerusalem, his crucifixion at the hands of the Romans. The cross became a symbol not only of Christianity, but also of the universal experience of spiritual death.

Can a person experience spiritual death more than once? I've fallen back into the pit a time or two. It's called Hell, and it isn't fun. But the second and third time you fall in, you have a memory of the first time you got out. The first time you fall in, you don't have any memory of getting out. There is no way out, until finally you find it. There's no memory because it hasn't happened before. That's what makes it so scary.

Depression, despair and mid-life crisis are spiritual experiences. The specifics vary with each individual. No one has the right to judge where others are in their spiritual journeys. You may understand yourself as spiritually innocent, never having known the pain of being in the bottomless pit where spiritual zombies live. You may feel worthless, unable even to hope for spiritual resurrection. You may begin to feel the hope of a new life. I believe that God loves people in all three categories equally. Being spiritually alive doesn't put you in a favored position with God, nor is it a position about which you can boast or brag.

Does this straw touch your clay? The next page is for your musings.

17. DEPRESSION, DESPAIR, MID-LIFE CRISIS, THE DEATH OF THE HUMAN SPIRIT: IS THAT A SPIRITUAL EVENT?

"Spiritual death" can be defined as the experience of despair, when one feels the absence of God, confronts one's own mortality in a profound way, and feels that life is meaningless and without purpose. This experience may be brief or may last for years.

What is the best example of spiritual death you can think of in literature or music, other than the death of Jesus?

Have you experienced spiritual death or are you experiencing it now? If so, what were/are the circumstances?

Have you experienced spiritual death more than once? If so, why? How many times? Do you expect more?

How do you think or feel your spiritual death relates to your physical death? Was/is it related to a profound encounter with your mortality?

CHAPTER 18
HOPE, METAMORPHOSIS, NEW LIFE, THE RESURRECTION OF THE HUMAN SPIRIT: IS THAT A SPIRITUAL EVENT?

Spiritual resurrection is the event or period of time when we move from spiritual death to spiritual life. It is the time of personal transformation. This is the metamorphosis moment. It is the most incredible miracle of all human experience, and it's the best thing you and God can do together.

Spiritual resurrection may be defined as finding life on the far side of despair, finding hope where there was none before, discovering the presence of God in new and more profound ways, coming to know a real sense of personal meaning and purpose. You have to fill in the specifics of these general definitions for yourself.

For some people, something clicks that was never there before, and the process begins. For others, there is a series of revelations of personal truths that clarify life. Some find the answer to the riddle that only they can solve. Others discover God and life in some unusual experience.

World literature is full of stories of spiritual resurrection. Motion pictures have been successes because they featured someone's resurrection as the climactic moment.

> *Star Wars* **presents several characters who experience spiritual death and resurrection, but none as graphic as the character known as Darth Vader. He was trained to be a Jedi, an ardent participant in The Force and all that was good, but along the way he was turned to the Dark Side. He became the most cruel warrior of the fearsome Empire, inflicting pain on many in the Rebel Alliance, including his own daughter, Princess Leia and son, Luke Skywalker. In the end, when forced to witness Luke's torture by the evil Emperor, he leaves the Dark Side, kills the Emperor and reconciles with his son, just before he dies. The pivotal event of the Hebrew Bible is the escape of the Israelites from Egypt under the leadership of Moses, the tortuous time in the various wildernesses of the Sinai peninsula and eventual entrance into the Promised Land, which is the spiritual death and resurrection theme. The nation of Israel is depicted as the spiritual adolescent in slavery in Egypt, followed by the spiritual young adult in confusion and despair in the wilderness. Crossing the Jordan and entering and conquering the Promised Land is symbolic of attaining mature spiritual adulthood and new life in partnership with God.**

The central point of the New Testament is the spiritual death and resurrection of Jesus. This was discussed in Chapter 9. The essence of Jesus is not found in his birth, his baptism, his temptations, his transfiguration, his teachings, his miracles, his physical death or his physical resurrection. That could all go away. What will never go away is that Jesus is God's great universal symbol of the universal fact of spiritual death and the universal hope of spiritual resurrection.

One of the common themes of this oft-repeated story of spiritual death and resurrection is that life is radically different than before. However, "they lived happily ever after" only happens in fairy tales. Spiritual life is not a continuous matter, though it is forever. There are times when the great metamorphosis is forgotten and irrelevant. But, when memory returns, new life returns.

> **A leading Pharisee named Nicodemus came to see Jesus one night and said to him, "Rabbi, it's obvious that you're a teacher who has come from God. You couldn't have done the things you've been doing unless you experience the presence of God."**
>
> **Jesus answered him, "I'm telling you the truth when I tell you that no one can experience the Kingdom of Heaven without experiencing spiritual birth."**
>
> **Nicodemus said to him, "How can a grown person be birthed a second time? You can't crawl back into your mother's womb and be born again."**
>
> **Jesus answered, "That's very true, but no one can experience the Kingdom of God who has not experienced being claimed by God and who has not experienced spiritual birth. Physical birth is physical birth, but spiritual birth is spiritual resurrection. You look a little amazed that I said that you have to experience spiritual birth. God's breath of life is self-directed and you don't control where it goes or to whom it goes. So anyone who experiences spiritual birth cannot claim credit for it" (John 3:1-8, paraphrased).**

It seems that Nicodemus began to understand that he needed to acknowledge that he was accepted by God. It is amazing that this knowledge, given to him by Jesus, quickly pointed toward the wisdom in Jesus' words, namely that spiritual birth comes as people touch God and as God touches people, in as many ways as people understand the nature of God.

You can see this idea working in the lowly caterpillar. The caterpillar labors long and hard to make a cocoon around itself and finally closes the door. Inside the protective environment, miraculous changes take place. What was fuzzy becomes gossamer wings. What was plain becomes spectacular. And then the time comes to break out. It's a hard struggle, a painful process. Breaking out of the cocoon is fraught with the fear that you may not make it, and indeed some don't. Some die trying. Some quit and die without trying. But the victorious new creature works hard, building up muscles. It cracks the hard surface and fights to emerge. If a human tries to help it break out, the butterfly may never fly, because it needs the struggle to prepare itself for life outside the cocoon. When it emerges, it spreads its wings and begins a life it has never known before, but a life that it has always hoped for.

I had died trying to be perfect, morally and ethically perfect. I realized I was getting nowhere. But that was my goal. That was the meaning and purpose of life to me. Then one day, I said to myself, "I really don't feel good about life. In fact, I'm miserable. I'm not enjoying life. There's no joy in Mudville." And so, I quit. I resigned from the human race, convinced that God didn't love me, that God just watched me to catch me when I did wrong. I said, "If that's God, there is no God." I blew that God off.

There I was, a little Baptist boy in Mississippi College, deader than doornails spiritually, and reading Jean-Paul Sartre. I was majoring in French literature. I was reading *L'Etre et le Neant (Being and Nothingness)* in French, a 700-page tome by Sartre. Sartre was an atheist, communist, humanist, existentialist Frenchman, but Sartre wrote the words which are to me the very essence of Christian theology, "Life begins on the far side of despair." Sartre became a Catholic before he died. If he made it to the far side of despair is not for me to judge. But, he helped me a lot.

While I was in the depths of hell, wishing I could get out, I had a vision of a spark of the love of God for me. I remembered that experience of my Daddy looking for me in two feet of snow in Edinburgh, and I wondered if God might be looking for me now in the depths of hell. I began to think that there may be a loving God who doesn't watch everything I do in the bathtub, who doesn't zap me with lightning when I do something rather innocent, but who accepts me as an imperfect human being and loves me unconditionally.

I began clawing my way toward that hope of a concept of God. That was the beginning of my spiritual resurrection. The first day of my new life, I walked out of Chrestman Hall, my college dormitory, and actually paid attention to another human being for the first time in my adult life. That was significant, because up until then I had only paid attention to myself in my quest for moral perfection. And because I believed previously that life here and now was not important, compared to the life in heaven, I had paid attention to the future but not the present. I began learning how to concentrate on life in the here and now. I began learning the importance of paying attention to other people. I became a great deal less self-conscious doing that, and my life-stress level dropped dramatically.

> I started having fun. I loosened up a little bit and it was pretty amazing. I began reflecting on faith matters in a new way. I looked at my old beliefs about Jesus, especially my sworn beliefs about the physical resurrection of Jesus on Easter, and concluded that it was not of supreme importance that the physical resurrection happened. I began to look at the physical resurrection as a symbol of something greater and grander, namely the spiritual resurrection of Jesus.

After Paul of Tarsus died spiritually on the road to Damascus, he was baptized and ministered to by Christians in Damascus, and then he went out into the desert to ponder what had happened to him, to rebuild his own theology, and to be spiritually resurrected. After Peter died spiritually when Jesus was crucified, he began his spiritual resurrection on Easter morning when he encountered, in vivid fashion, new life and new hope, meaning and purpose, all symbolized by an empty tomb.

Jeremiah died spiritually in the bottom of an empty cistern in Jerusalem. Then a eunuch from the king's court came along and threw him a rope, thus beginning his rescue from the bottomless pit and his spiritual resurrection.

Jacob died spiritually in the face of sudden death at the hands of his brother, Esau. As he crawled on his belly toward his brother and his death, Esau showed him a new concept of God. Jacob saw in Esau a loving, forgiving and compassionate God. Jacob's name was changed to Israel. His concept of God was changed. His spiritual resurrection had begun.

Abraham died spiritually when told to sacrifice his only son, Isaac, to God. As he was about to slit the boy's throat, God stopped him, provided a ram for the sacrifice, and Abraham's spiritual resurrection began.

Here's the bottom line. If you are in your spiritual innocence, enjoy it. If you are spiritually dead, there is life on the far side of despair. If you are spiritually alive, you have a great responsibility to live your life each day to the fullest, in the presence of God in the Kingdom of Heaven.

Where are you?

18. HOPE, METAMORPHOSIS, NEW LIFE, THE RESURRECTION OF THE HUMAN SPIRIT: IS THAT A SPIRITUAL EVENT?

"Spiritual resurrection" may be defined as finding life on the far side of despair, finding hope where there was none before, discovering the presence of God in new and more profound ways, coming to know a real sense of personal meaning and purpose.

What is the best example of spiritual resurrection you can think of in literature or music, other than the resurrection of Jesus?

Have you experienced spiritual resurrection, or are you experiencing it now? If yes, what were/are the circumstances and what did/does it feel like?

What new meaning and purpose have you acknowledged in your life as a result of spiritual resurrection?

Is there any connection between spiritual life after spiritual resurrection and your concept of heaven?

CHAPTER 19
IS IT TIME TO FIRE YOUR OLD GOD?

You worked like fury to make the bucks, buy the house, trade in the cars, have the babies, earn the raises, get the promotions. Now you find that it all rusts and needs painting again. You want to give up the chase but what would you replace it with? You suspect that God would tell you if you knew how to listen. You want peace and serenity. You want the kind of beauty that cannot be bought. You want a purpose. You want to be a better person. You want to love more fully and with less self-interest. You believe, in some deep, quiet place within you, that God can give you all that.

You may be tired of feeling guilty before God. You may not want to be bound anymore by other people's rules and ideas. You may not want to become nutty and weird. You may not want to live a joyless life. You may not want more expectations and obligations than you can meet. You may not want to be turned into the kind of person who mouths pieties and speaks in holy jargon.

You could believe that God is such a clumsy creator or so inept at transformation that God is trying to force you into being someone other than yourself. You might believe that God is only as other people see God, or that God is only as you see God, or that there is only one concept of the nature of God. This last thought may cause you to think that the God you believed in at age six or 16 or 60 is the one you must force yourself to believe in the rest of your life.

One of the most damaging misunderstandings about the nature of God is that God is the same for everyone. The parable of the blind men and the elephant shows that you believe in the part of God you can touch, but you can't touch all the parts. As you go through life, you may often change your ideas about God as you experience new things and build your personal faith with a passion. That means you may have to fire your old God and hire a new one.

You need the clay of your own experience to make the belief bricks of personal faith. In working with that clay, you learn that experience is spiritually valid. Your experiences validate your faith. It is important to acknowledge your experiences and what it means to you about God.

> **Daddy took me with him to the hardware, feed and seed store in Tylertown one spring day. I was six years old. While he was hunting whatever he needed, I stood at the front counter, near a bag of seed corn. It feels so good to run seed corn through your fingers.**
>
> **Being springtime in the deep South, it was hot outside and my hands were sweaty. Unbeknownst to me, two kernels of seed corn stuck to my palm and wound up in my pocket. When we got home, I discovered my sin. I had stolen two kernels of seed corn from the Tylertown Hardware, Feed and Seed store, though I hadn't meant to.**

Overcome with guilt, but determined not to be found out, I undid the latch on the dining room window screen and furtively dropped those two kernels on the ground outside. Our house didn't have gutters. There was a trough on that side of the house where the rainwater fell off the roof. The items I had stolen came to rest in that trough.

As the spring progressed, two stalks began to rise past the dining room window sill. It became the topic of conversation each evening at the dinner table. The rest of the family thought it some sort of miracle. I refused to look at the evidence of my sin.

As spring turned into summer, ears of corn appeared on both stalks. The table conversation turned to when the ears would be ripe unto harvest. One summer day, during a thunderstorm, Daddy was standing at the window, drooling over the prospects of eating that home-grown corn, when a bolt of lightning struck a tree on that side of the house, bounced over and fried both corn stalks and shocked Daddy.

When I heard what had happened, I knew that God had rendered judgment on me for my sin of stealing. I lived for a long time in mortal fear of accidentally taking anything that didn't belong to me. The idea of intentionally stealing anything from anybody was not even in the realm of possibility. The God of Judgment had my number and was watching my every move.

Plenty of folks will be ready to tell you that you don't have the authority to know whether God really is as your experience tells you God is. Some theologians and some clergy may be especially eager to tell you that you must accept their experiences and ideas. Lay people of all faiths will also be willing to dispute your beliefs. That's all right. They don't have to believe what you do. But you may have to let go of some of the ways you once believed in order to embrace your new growing faith. It won't be easy, but what you're doing is exactly what the Apostle Paul did. It's what Augustine did. It's what many great religious leaders have done to reach God in new and deeper ways.

But you may desperately need the great intangible gifts that God has made available to you since you were born. God's love, peace of mind, calmness of spirit, patience, and wisdom are but a few of the gifts at your disposal on a daily basis as you make your belief bricks and build your spiritual house of faith. The trick is to learn your personal way of accepting these gifts and using them and passing them on. It takes courage to fire your old God and hire a new God.

You can make marks on the graph on the next page that shows what your experience tells you about the nature of God. The graph uses fifteen attributes of God that go from positive to negative. For instance, you pick a point between loving and apathetic, a point between caring and judging, a point between forgiving and blaming, etc. Then you can answer for yourself whether God has gender and whether God has an abiding place. It continues the discussion of emotions engendered as you think about God.

19. IS IT TIME TO FIRE YOUR OLD GOD?

The following are spectra, continua, ranges, scales. Mark a place on each line that applies to your concept, at the point on the line that fits your concept.

Loving ———————————————————————— Apathetic

Caring ———————————————————————— Judging

Forgiving ———————————————————————— Blaming

Accepting ———————————————————————— Demanding

Freeing ———————————————————————— Controlling

Hearing ———————————————————————— Ignoring

Revealing ———————————————————————— Concealing

Creating ———————————————————————— Destroying

Active ———————————————————————— Passive

Patient ———————————————————————— Angry

Dynamic ———————————————————————— Static

Kind ———————————————————————— Mean

Fair ———————————————————————— Capricious

Honest ———————————————————————— Dishonest

Immanent ———————————————————————— Transcendent

Also, in your concept of the nature of God, is God —

❏ Male ❏ Female ❏ Gender neutral ❏ Gender language doesn't matter

❏ In Heaven ❏ On Earth ❏ Everywhere ❏ Place doesn't matter

SECTION E

ALLOWING YOUR BELIEF BRICKS
TO EXPRESS THEMSELVES

Building a spiritual house of faith is a means to an end, not an end in itself. The purpose of molding bricks and constructing a house is to create a faith that naturally expresses itself. That faith may be expressed in written form, if you are comfortable with writing. It may be expressed in spoken form, if you are comfortable talking about it. It may be expressed in art forms if you are an artist. Your faith should be so important to you that it cries out to be expressed.

There are eighteen steps to living life at its very best:

1. Recognize that you don't know what you believe about God as well as you would like and have difficulty expressing what you believe to others.

2. Do an inventory of your life experiences and identify the experiences when you felt the presence or absence of God. (Evoke clay)

3. Reflect on those experiences to determine what they meant to you, consciously or unconsciously, about the nature of God, at the time the experiences occurred. (Inspect clay)

4. Keep a log for one week of what you do, why you do it, and how you do it in order to identify your unconscious faith at work. (Examine clay)

5. Reflect on what your log tells you about who you are and what it says about your present concept of the nature of God. (Evaluate clay)

6. Make a list of the most significant spiritual teachings you have received by reading, listening and/or watching. (Identify straw)

7. Determine which significant teachings you agree with and which you disagree with. (Divide straw)

8. Match the agreeable teachings with your life experiences that relate to those teachings. (Mix straw and clay)

9. Express in your own way what this mixture means about your present concept of the nature of God. (Make bricks and claim them)

10. Look and listen for the presence or absence of God in the experiences of each day. (Add clay)

11. Look and listen for more teachings that match your life experiences. (Collect more straw)

12. Reflect consciously on the meaning of the experiences and the validity of the teachings in your experience, and express that meaning in your own way. (Make more bricks and claim them)

13. Arrange these expressions in some fashion that is orderly from your perspective, and that tells you as clearly as possible what you believe right now about God. (Build your house of faith)

14. Look for the connection between what you believe about God and who you are or who you want to become. If you believe at this point in a loving God, then . . .

15. Love yourself more as you understand yourself better and as you accept yourself more easily, with the belief that you are totally accepted by God.

16. Love others more with a love that overflows from within.

17. Love God, with unconditional acceptance of your concept of the nature of God.

18. Live life at its best, fullest, richest, most meaningful level.

Most importantly, your conscious faith, your personal faith, should be expressed in the way you live your life each day. When your actions are a result of a conscious and consistent faith, you have integrity, meaning and purpose in your life. If you have children or grandchildren, they will read, hear and see your faith. They are looking at your face to see the face of God in a symbolic way. This can be the greatest influence on them as they build their own houses of faith in later years. Your belief bricks will be important straw for them.

CHAPTER 20
HOW CAN YOU CONSCIOUSLY EXPRESS WHAT YOU BELIEVE ABOUT THE NATURE OF GOD?

Now it's time to pull it all together into one piece, to see how the bricks are stacking up into a structure, your spiritual house of faith. I encourage you to look for consistencies and inconsistencies, parallels or contradictions between one brick and another. For example, does your concept of God allow you to favor the pro-life position and favor capital punishment simultaneously? Or, to reverse the equation, does your concept of God allow you to favor the pro-choice position and be opposed to capital punishment simultaneously?

Turning to another ethical issue, does your concept of God permit the condemnation of homosexuality while winking at marital infidelity? Or, on the other hand, does your concept of God permit the acceptance of homosexuality and insistence on husbands and wives being faithful to one another?

Does your concept of God include forgiveness for bad choices, accidents AND evil acts? Do you always experience God in the same way or in different ways? Have you solved for yourself the "problem" of Jesus and how Jesus relates to God? What is your answer to the question of the relationship between Holy Spirit and God? Is the Bible a literary god or a book of faith for you?

These are just a few ways to compare your bricks to make sure there is integrity in your spiritual house of faith. Take the time to think through your belief bricks before you begin your expressions of faith, otherwise you will be sending out garbled and confusing messages, expressions without integrity or passion.

Here is one person's written expression of faith:

> "I see God today as a kind and loving God. He is not the Santa Claus I want him to be. He doesn't buy me cars, give me money, or get me jobs. He does give me the strength to get those things for myself. I don't think he cares very much about what kind of car I drive, or what kind of house I live in, or what kind of job I have. He does care about what makes me happy and he wants me to have everything that will make me happy.
>
> "One of God's best gifts is the gift of clarity. I have insight today that I didn't used to have. I see and comprehend things today that used to pass me by. I see a bigger picture than I used to.
>
> "Another gift is that I am now able to feel. Nine years ago I was completely numb. I was not able to cry when I hurt nor when I felt joy. Today I cry at both. . . .
>
> "Anyway I do feel God today more than I ever have. I connect at least once a day and most days several times. Most of my days are peaceful and most of the time my mind is peaceful. That's a big deal." — Mandy Downs, Montgomery, AL

Does your verbal expression of faith have integrity, or are there contradictions within it? It is important that your belief bricks fit together at critical points. However, your experiences and your hopes are the most accurate validators of your belief bricks.

Now, after an intense period of introspection and hard work to sort through the faith options and choose for yourself what will be your faith, it's time to turn your eyeballs around and look out at the world and the human race and express your faith in the many ways faith can be expressed. In other words, **IF IT ISN'T GOING THROUGH YOU, IT ISN'T GETTING TO YOU.**

Personal faith with a passion is like a wire conducting electricity. It has to pass through you to others. If it stops with you, the electricity shorts out and a fuse is blown. The end result of knowing what you really believe is not to sit alone in your spiritual house of faith, but to go out of that house each day you can to express your faith in conscious ways. Your spiritual house of faith will serve as your base camp for climbing the mountain every day.

Another way to say it is: **YOU ONLY GET TO KEEP WHAT YOU GIVE AWAY.** If you sit on your faith, you lose. If you express your faith, you win. You get to keep it. If you give away what you believe, you are throwing your straw in the wind, and the wind may carry it to people who need your straw. God can show up in a clear revelatory manner when you stop sitting around waiting for God and start doing what you believe God wishes you would do. This step is critical for you if you want God to keep communicating to you and if you want to strengthen your faith by living it. You lose whatever you hoard, including your money, your love, your joy.

Finding the freedom to gather your own straw and believe in your own experiences takes courage. Affirming your freedom to gather your own straw and confidence in the validity of your experiences pose another danger. You have to walk a fine line. Now you're acting on what you believe God is revealing to you, not to anyone else, just to you.

One of the great dangers of spiritual life is thinking that you are acting under God's direct orders and being completely mistaken. Some of the evil that's been done in the world has been done in the name of God. There are ways to avoid falling into the trap of misguided righteousness. When God seems to be saying that the end justifies the means, watch out. You can find plenty of straw and clay to keep you on the right track if you resist the temptation to think too highly of yourself.

Often you don't know what spiritual truth you're discovering until the end of the process. Only then can you articulate what you believe and begin testing it. Now your faith becomes visible. Without this step, you cannot truly grow.

You often know that the belief bricks are solid enough by the sense of awe, peace or joy that your newly recognized faith gives. Sometimes, however, you know it by the way your life is changing. You know it by the fact that you find yourself becoming the person you want very much to be. This completes your spiritual house of faith and allows you to express what you believe.

When you are on your game, you are living out and acting out who and what you believe God to be. When you do that consciously, there is great integrity in your life. When you do that unconsciously, you are also living out what your unconscious faith says about God. The danger is that you may be hypocritical if what you say you believe and what you do don't match.

Here is another written statement of personal faith by a person who is trying to live by faith, telling how her life has changed because of this new direction.

> **"I believe in one God whose love for me and everything known and unknown to me is powerful, unconditional and unwavering. God is my hope, my guide, my salvation. Without God I am nothing. I do not fear God in the modern sense of the word "fear" because love transcends fear. God lives through me. God is energized by the love flowing out from me.**
>
> **"I believe Jesus is of God as all mortals are of God. Everything about his life and teachings are not known to us and what is known is open to interpretation. Jesus accepted God's gift of love that is available to all of us, but it was on a level that we find difficult to sustain. It is my belief that Jesus' death symbolizes and offers us the hope of spiritual death and resurrection. When I really think about Jesus, I weep from the depths of my soul.**
>
> **"God uses the Holy Spirit to communicate with me, to serve as my inner voice. When faced with great sadness and despair, when the world is more than I can handle alone, I pray to God for love to fill my soul. Only when I am full of God's love and let that love flow through me can I fully enjoy the richness of life."** — Nan Gray, Oklahoma City

There is an important verse in the prophecy of Habakkuk which was quoted and emphasized by the apostle Paul, St. Augustine and the Protestant reformers, which says, "Those who know how to live, live by faith"(Habakkuk 2:4). Those who know how to live express their faith on a daily basis, in word and deed, written and oral and intentional. They may express their faith in artistic endeavors if they are gifted in the arts. They express their faith in their attitude toward life in general, and, specifically, toward family, friends, co-workers, community members, and the list goes on.

Those who know how to live express their faith in the quest for justice and fairness in society. They have causes about which they care deeply. Not only do they vote in elections but they often get involved in the political process, campaigning for candidates they believe can make our society more just and fair. They often find a way to be involved in a humanitarian effort, from animal shelters to feeding the hungry. They are usually as generous as possible in their giving to charitable organizations, supporting causes in which they believe with their money.

You have your ways to express your faith in a conscious manner. How much richer it is to live out your faith and know why you're doing what you're doing!

20. HOW CAN YOU CONSCIOUSLY EXPRESS WHAT YOU BELIEVE ABOUT THE NATURE OF GOD?

In your own words, based on all your answers in this book, write what you believe at this time in your life about the nature of God . . . who and/or what God is to you today.

CHAPTER 21
HOW CAN YOU EXPRESS YOUR FAITH TO CHILDREN?

If you have children or grandchildren, they are looking right in your face to see what the face of God looks like. They will see in you God-like qualities, for good or ill. If you teach or coach children, what they experience interacting with you will be a part of their clay for the rest of their lives.

It is so important to know what you believe and to express your faith to children, in word and deed, with honesty and integrity. In other words, tell them what you believe, but also tell them what you wonder about and what you don't know. You cannot give them your belief bricks, but you can give them straw that is based on your belief bricks.

Tell children your faith stories. Describe to them the clay, your experiences, that you used to make your belief bricks. Reveal to them the straw that made a real difference to you as you did your faith-building. Be honest about those aspects of your faith that are based on your hopes and dreams. Tell them the truth and don't mislead them as many well-meaning parents have done in the past. Let them know their clay is and will be different from yours, and their straw will be different from yours, so their belief bricks will be different from yours. That's the way it should be. Give children the same freedom to build their houses of faith that you are enjoying.

Each of the last four generations of Americans has been more insistent on thinking for themselves about spiritual matters than the previous generation. Baby Boomers are more insistent than Builders. Generation X is less likely to follow blindly than Baby Boomers. The Millennial Generation is looking for newer ways of thinking about everything. All of this is a matter of degrees of separation, not a cataclysmic shift, but there are fewer children today who will take the faith of someone else as Truth for them.

Let's reverse the equation. What do the children have to tell you about faith? First, they have their stories. Invite them to tell you their faith stories. Ask them when and where they met God or God-like people or experienced awesome moments when they felt the presence or absence of God. Here's the kind of story you may hear.

> **A little boy wanted to meet God. He knew it was a long trip to where God lived, so he packed his suitcase with Twinkies and a six-pack of Coca-Cola and started off. He had walked quite a distance when he passed a park, where he saw an old man sitting on a bench, staring at the pigeons. The boy was getting tired and hungry, so he sat down next to the old man and opened the suitcase.**
>
> **He was about to take a drink from his Coke when he noticed that the old man looked hungry, so he offered him a Twinkie. The old man accepted it gratefully, and smiled at the boy, though he did not speak. His smile was so pleasant that the boy wanted to see it again, so he offered him a Coke. Again, the old man smiled. The boy was delighted.**

> They sat there a long time eating Twinkies and drinking Cokes and smiling, but they never said a word. As the afternoon shadows grew longer, the boy realized how tired he was and he got up to leave, but before he had gone more than a few steps, he turned around, ran back to the old man, and gave him a hug. The old man smiled the biggest smile ever.
>
> When the boy opened the door to his own house a short time later, his mother was surprised by the look of joy on his face. She asked him, "What did you do today that made you so happy?
>
> He replied, "I had lunch with God." Before his mother could respond, he added, "you know what? He's got the most beautiful smile I've ever seen!"
>
> Meanwhile, the old man returned to the home of his son, where he lived. His son was stunned by the look of peace on his face and asked, "Dad, what did you do today that made you so happy?"
>
> The old man said, "I ate Twinkies and drank Cokes in the park with God." Before his son could reply, the old man added: "And you know, he's much younger that I expected."
> (Author unknown)

Secondly, listen carefully to the children as they tell their stories. If it is appropriate, help them find the meaning in the experiences they relate in their stories. Don't tell children that they didn't experience what they say they experienced. Guide them with questions toward their understanding the depth of a holy moment, an awesome experience, a God time.

Thirdly, encourage children to find the spiritual symbols in the movies and TV shows they see. In Chapter 3, I told you about a group of fifth through eighth-graders that I worked with. After showing them how to pull out spiritual symbols from movies, they could do it on their own with a sense of pride and accomplishment. They worked with me on faith-building for four hours on a Saturday afternoon in a camp setting. Their leaders were astonished that they were so attentive and interested to spend that kind of time doing faith stuff with so much to play with all around them. My comment to their leaders was that children are interested in dealing with matters of faith that are important TO THEM. When expressing your faith to children, remember to do it using their agenda, not yours.

> Marty and Tamara are both attorneys. They have two boys, Stephen and Brooks. They wanted to tell their children what they believed but they hesitated, knowing that they weren't sure what they believed. They participated in a workshop on "Personal Faith with a Passion," and they began building their houses of faith.

They have worked hard to mold bricks and build their faith. They are ecstatic about being able to answer their boys' faith questions. They no longer feel that they have to take Stephen and Brooks to a religious professional for faith discussions, even though they are regular church-goers. They deal with issues of faith in their home.

Children need to receive good religious information from their parents. Books and religious institutions are also available to provide the straw which children can use early in life to form belief bricks and even more so as they grow older. Bricks formed in early life are primarily about values, and values are important for children and adolescents.

EPILOGUE

WHAT DO YOU BELIEVE SO PASSIONATELY THAT YOU WOULD GIVE UP EVERYTHING YOU OWN FOR IT RIGHT NOW?

Passion is the key word. Unless you are passionate about your faith, it doesn't mean much to you or anybody else. The main reason why American Christianity is growing more and more anemic in the 21st Century is that most American Christians have a secondhand faith and don't know what they personally believe. The second reason for this anemia is the lack of passion about a faith they didn't work to construct. It's hard to get excited about somebody else's faith.

Passion about your faith should not lead you to be spiritually arrogant but spiritually humble. Passion is what makes you act on your faith. Passion is what brings integrity to faith. Passion makes your spiritual house of faith alive, a great place to live, and a warm, inviting place for guests to come with their straw to give and gather straw to take away with them. Passion also makes your house of faith a good base from which to go out into the world to tell and show and do your faith.

Christianity was born in Jerusalem and Rome and Alexandria and Antioch and Ephesus, cities where early Jesus followers had to decide what they believed so passionately that they would give up everything they owned for it right then, because many of them lost everything they owned. Indeed, many of them lost their lives at the hands of the Romans for what they believed. But, it was the strength and depth of their faith, demonstrating their passion, that caused others to want to develop a faith that made that much difference in their lives.

Fear and guilt and a hope for a better existence in the next life have been the primary motivators of Christianity since the early days. Love should be the great motivator of Christianity. In the process of building your spiritual house of faith, your love for yourself and those around you and your love for the God of your understanding should grow. That's where the passion should come from: LOVE. On the last day of your physical life on this planet, what will count as most important will be how much love and how much resulting joy you experienced in your days. Let the passion flow!

POSTSCRIPT

Why do you need to spend your time and energy building personal faith with a passion?

1. When you know what you believe, then you can know who you are, then you can love yourself, then you can love others, then you can love God, then you can live life as wished by God.

2. The better you know what you believe, the better you know who you are. You need self-understanding, a healthy self-concept, a positive identity, and your faith is your key to all that.

3. When your conscious faith has integrity with the way you live your life, you have meaning and purpose in your life.

4. With a carefully constructed spiritual house, you can handle the crises of life and grow in them.

5. In the process of building your personal faith, you learn the true, profound meaning of freedom and responsibility. When you know that you have the freedom to build and rebuild your own house of faith, you know you must give others the same freedom. When you build your personal faith, you know that it is your responsibility to "work out (your) salvation with fear and trembling," (Philippians 2:12) in partnership with God, one day at a time.

6. When you experience the difficulty of building your own spiritual house, you learn the real meaning of humility and you cannot be theologically arrogant toward another pilgrim.

At issue is your identity, your effectiveness as a human being, your ability to establish covenant relationships, your ability to cope with the best and the worst of life, your knowing the meaning and purpose of your life, your freedom and responsibility, and your ability to walk humbly with your God and family and friends. In short, your spiritual life is at issue. There is nothing more important than your spiritual life. Building your personal faith is the most important thing you will ever do. That makes this task worth doing.

> If and when you grow weary of building your personal faith,
> come back and read the answers to this question.

INDEX OF STORIES AND ILLUSTRATIONS

Joe the Quarterback 14
Paul and Personal Faith with a Passion 18
Augustine and Personal Faith with a Passion 18
Henry's Spiritual Photo Album 21
Dr. Hyatt as a God Image 25
Eston Myers as a Saint 26
Woman Abused by Her Father 27
"Squeaky" as a God Image 27
The Face of God in the Snow of Edinburgh 28
Easter Sunrise Service 33
Cathedral of the Grand Canyon 33
Death of Rocky Fellow 34
Bombings and Terrorist Attacks 34
Decision to Try a New Form of Ministry 35
Caught Being a Horse's Ass 36
Clyde Cromwell and the Cricket 37
God Watching in the Bathroom 37
Poseidon Adventure 41
Jacob's Transformation 42
Lash LaRue 45
Donald Clark and the Freudian Slip 49
Two Scottish Boys 50
Electrician Praying for the Pastor 51
Valerie Love and the Wrong Number 52
Three Fishermen and Their Prayer 54
Martha and Jim and the Tragedy of Faith 61
Sunday School Contest 62
Two Women Thinking for Themselves 64
Worm and Wretch 67
Feeding the Coachwhip Snake 73
Bible as Autobiography 78
Reclining Couches 79

Dionysus	88
Jesus as Balloon in Macy's Parade	91
Jesus' Baptism	92
Jesus' Temptation	92
Jesus' Spiritual Death and Psalm 22	94
Jesus' Spiritual Resurrection	96
Jesus' Transfiguration	96
Friend Stopped Breathing	101
Snake Handling	102
Margie the Atheist	113
Oklahoma City Bombing and the Will of God	114
Call to Ministry	115
Tolerance in Faith is a Virtue	119
Alternative Version of Garden of Eden Story	121
Six Blind People and the Elephant	125
Ten Commandments or Thirteen Words?	129
Battle of Armageddon	137
Heaven and Hell	141
Daddy Finds Himself in Hell	142
Living in the Kingdom of Heaven	144
Ralph's Mother Dies – Heaven or Holding Tank?	146
What if This is Heaven Promised in Last Life?	147
Karen, Josh and Sam – Spiritual Death	151
Spiritual Death of Biblical Characters	152
Star Wars and Spiritual Resurrection	157
Nicodemus and Jesus on Spiritual Rebirth	158
Personal Spiritual Death and Resurrection	159
Two Kernels of Seed Corn	163
Mandy Downs' Expression of Faith	169
Nan Gray's Expression of Faith	171
Little Boy and Old Man Who Met God	175
Marty and Tamara and Their Children	176

Notes:

The 3 Little Pigs Revisited:
How to Build Your Spiritual House of Faith

The 3 Little Pigs Revisited is a book by Dr. Dykes that presents a modified version of the famous fairy tale by the Brothers Grimm as a modern parable. It clarifies the introduction to *Personal Faith with a Passion*, explaining in simple language the importance of combining your experiences with religious information to create personal faith. The story is illustrated in graphic drawings by Ty Flippo, which makes this book a joy for children and teens as well as adults.

The importance of this little book is that it makes available to everyone a proven technique which can be used to build your faith in your own way. *The 3 Little Pigs Revisited* can be seen as a precursor to this book, and its reading may encourage people to read *Personal Faith with a Passion*.

To order *The Three Little Pigs Revisited: How to Build Your Spiritual House of Faith,*

1. Send check or money order for $9.95, plus $2.00 for shipping and handling, to:
    Pair'o'Docs Press
    9205 Lansbrook Lane
    Oklahoma City, OK, 73132
2. Telephone order to 405-728-2833 and provide information on MasterCard or VISA

To order additional copies of *Personal Faith with a Passion: How to Know What You Really Believe* to give as gifts to family and friends, the price is $18.50, plus $2.00 shipping and handling. (For sales within Oklahoma, add $1.50 sales tax.)

Notes:

DR. RAY DYKES
and the
PERSONAL FAITH PROGRAM

The Personal Faith Program offers a full range of pastoral services to you when you choose Dr. Dykes as your personal pastor.

1. Personal spiritual coaching. Sometimes you need to reflect privately with a theological professional on what you believe and don't believe. Dr. Dykes coaches you on how to pull your faith out of your experiences. This one-to-one time may be the piece that makes possible your transition to a more complete personal identity. Telephone sessions are available for those around the country.

2. General pastoral services. Dr. Dykes calls on the phone and makes personal visits to encourage you in your spiritual journey. He prays with and for you, especially upon your request. Wedding and funeral services are provided. Referrals are made to the best physical and mental healthcare professionals in the area. Dr. Dykes also visits in hospitals when participants inform him of their hospitalization. These services are available only in OKC.

3. Small group gatherings. Groups gather in homes on weekday evenings for religious information sharing on a variety of subjects. The major purpose of this sharing time is to help you build your faith in a form that function for you and provides you with meaning and purpose in life. (OKC only)

4. Pastoral care in the major crises of life. Dr. Dykes is available to be with those in Oklahoma City in emergency life situations, around the clock and seven days a week. In the worst of times, you may need a trusted, caring and non-judging pastor to be with you.

5. Theological writings. Dr. Dykes produces short articles on pertinent matters of theology as often as possible. So far, he has written four books, Unigospel, The Story in the Torah, The Three Little Pigs Revisited and Personal Faith with a Passion. The articles are distributed to you by fax, email, regular mail, personal delivery and on our website. These articles and books encourage you to think about your faith.

For additional information about the Personal Faith Program,
        call Dr. Dykes at 728.2844 or
          e-mail at raydykes@personalpastor.org or
        go to homepage www.personalpastor.org

Notes:

WORKSHOPS

Dr. Dykes conducts workshops in churches and public places on Personal Faith with a Passion. From 1996 to 2003, he conducted workshops in the following cities:

Green Valley, Arizona
Fort Smith, Arkansas
Athens, Georgia
Houston, Texas
Dallas, Texas
Ft. Worth, Texas
Oklahoma City, Oklahoma
Duncan, Oklahoma
Edmond, Oklahoma
Norman, Oklahoma
Columbus, Ohio
Greensboro, North Carolina
Detroit, Michigan
St. Louis, Missouri
Liberty, Missouri
Severna Park, Maryland
Paoli, Pennsylvania
Morrisville, Pennsylvania
Pittsburgh, Pennsylvania
Jackson, Mississippi
Virginia Beach, Virginia
Nashville, Tennessee

For information on how to arrange a workshop in your area, go to the web site of the Personal Faith Program, www.personalpastor.org or call 1-800-728-2844.

PUBLICATIONS AVAILABLE
from
the Personal Faith Program
and
Dr. Ray Dykes

UNIGOSPEL: A MERGING OF MATTHEW, MARK, LUKE
Merged, Blended & Arranged by Ray Dykes
January, 1996

> All the material in Matthew, Mark and Luke is presented in one document, eliminating duplication, and laying out the entire content in a logical, chronological and geographic-sensitive order. This is "the gospel for busy people," and for those who read the Bible for spiritual growth and pleasure. There is extensive use of the Scholars Version (SV), a product of the Jesus Seminar. This is a translation that tries to provide the reader what the listener may have heard when it was first said or read. Available for a contribution to the Personal Faith Program of $20, plus $2 for postage and handling if ordered.

THE STORY IN THE TORAH: AS TOLD IN THE BEGINNING
Translated, Paraphrased and/or Redacted by Ray Dykes
December, 1998

> This book was written for those people who want to understand the stories in the first five books of the Bible. It presents the ancient, unvarnished, tribal stories of the Hebrews in the same way the ancient Hebrews would have heard them, and later read them. Material not directly connected to the narrative material has been omitted. All the names of people and places have been translated or paraphrased, because Hebrew names meant something in the ears of the original listeners, and the meanings are essential to understanding the story. Available for a contribution to the Personal Faith Program of $20, plus $2 for postage and handling if ordered.

RELATING WORLD RELIGIONS TO CHRISTIANITY:
and details about some Christian Churches and a few Sect Groups
Compiled and Edited by Ray and Donna Dykes
September, 2001

> A workbook providing an overview and synopsis of some of the world's great religions and some major and minor Christian Churches and denominations. It focuses on the theology of these religions and churches, but also provides a quick peek at historical background, sacred book(s), organization, and distinctive practices. Each group is described in no more than two pages. Those described are: Hinduism,

Buddhism, Judaism, Zoroastrianism, Islam; Roman Catholicism, Eastern Orthodoxy, Lutheran, Presbyterian, Episcopal, Baptist, Methodist, Nazarene, Salvation Army, Christian Church (Disciples of Christ), Churches of Christ, Mormon, and Jehovah's Witnesses. Available for a contribution to the Personal Faith Program of $20, plus $2 for postage and handling if ordered.

PERSONAL AND CORPORATE FAITH SEEKING CONSCIOUS EXPRESSION: EARLY CHRISTIAN WRITINGS

Compiled and Edited by Ray Dykes

November, 1997

This booklet presents the expressed faith of early Christian writers, from Paul to Augustine. With one exception, the synopsis of information from each writer is presented in two pages, and includes biographical data, writings in existence, main contribution to the Christian movement, and expressions of faith in various theological categories. All the theology of these writers leads to or revolves around the writing of the Nicene Creed in 325 CE. The key issues are the nature of Jesus and the relationship between God and Jesus. Available for a contribution to the Personal Faith Program of $10, plus $2 for postage and handling if ordered.

To order any of these publications, provide your Name, Shipping Address, Phone Number and Payment Information to:

Personal Faith Program
9205 Lansbrook Lane
Oklahoma City, OK 73132

or e-mail to raydykes@personalpastor.org,
or phone 800.728.2844

Checks should be made payable to: Personal Faith Program
MasterCard and/or VISA is acceptable and information is secure.
If ordering by credit card, make sure you provide the Name (as imprinted on the card), Account Number and Expiration Date.

Thank you for your order! May you be blessed as you read!